Teaching Literacy in Urban Schools

Teaching Literacy in Urban Schools

Lessons from the Field

Edited by
Barbara Purdum-Cassidy
Lakia M. Scott

ROWMAN & LITTLEFIELD
Lanham • Boulder • New York • London

Published by Rowman & Littlefield
An imprint of The Rowman & Littlefield Publishing Group, Inc.
4501 Forbes Boulevard, Suite 200, Lanham, Maryland 20706
www.rowman.com

Unit A, Whitacre Mews, 26-34 Stannary Street, London SE11 4AB

British Library Cataloguing in Publication Information Available

Library of Congress Cataloging-in-Publication Data

Names: Purdum-Cassidy, Barbara, editor. | Scott, Lakia, editor.
Title: Teaching literacy in urban schools : lessons from the field / edited by Barbara Purdum-Cassidy, Lakia M. Scott.
Description: Lanham : Rowman & Littlefield, a wholly owned subsidiary of The Rowman & Littlefield Publishing Group, Inc., [2018] | Includes bibliographical references and index.
Identifiers: LCCN 2017049921 (print) | LCCN 2017059513 (ebook) | ISBN 9781475839340 (electronic) | ISBN 9781475839326 (cloth : alk. paper) | ISBN 9781475839333 (pbk. : alk. paper)
Subjects: LCSH: Language arts—Social aspects—United States. | City children—Education—United States. | Culturally relevant pedagogy—United States.
Classification: LCC LC5128 (ebook) | LCC LC5128 .T435 2018 (print) | DDC 372.6—dc23 LC record available at https://lccn.loc.gov/2017049921

Printed in the United States of America

Contents

Acknowledgments

I want to begin with special thanks to our editor, Sarah Jubar, who took a strong interest in this book. I am grateful for her enthusiasm, confidence, and belief in us. Thank you, Sarah, for your thoughtful feedback and encouragement during this process. I consider myself fortunate to have had the opportunity to work with such a supportive editor. I also want to thank the chapter authors for their contributions to this book. Their passion to improve literacy instruction in urban schools is reflected throughout this volume.

Next, I would like to thank my Baylor University colleagues for their dedication to our profession, and for how much they have inspired and taught me over the years. I am truly blessed to work at this wonderful university with such outstanding teacher educators. Heartfelt thanks go to my colleague, friend, and coeditor, Dr. Lakia M. Scott. I am grateful for our collaboration and look forward to our future endeavors.

This book would not have been possible without the love and support of my husband, Dan. You bring such joy to my life and remind me daily what is most important. Finally, to my children—Shannon, Courtney, and Tanner. Thank you for your love, patience, and encouragement.

—Barbara Purdum-Cassidy

Psalms 20:4 states, *May He give you the desires of your heart and make your plans succeed.* In prayer and devotion, this book was accomplished. Thank you, Lord. I must also give thanks for my family—my husband, Chadwick, and son, Chadley, along with my parents (Paul and Collette Jones) and in-laws (Cecil and Pamela Thomas). All have been incredibly understanding and supportive of my academic and career pursuits—for that I am forever grateful.

Next, I would like to thank my Baylor University faculty colleagues and administrators for consistently providing guidance, support, and advocacy for endeavors such as these. We always joke about "solving all the world's problems," but I truly believe that with such an impassioned group of colleagues, we will transform educational practice for the better. I also express my sincere appreciation to Dr. Barbara Purdum-Cassidy, the coeditor of this project. Your dedication to our students and program continue to encourage and excite me about teaching and learning.

Finally, heartfelt thanks to our contributing authors, who worked tirelessly with Barbara and me for the manifestation of this project. Let us continue to go forth and do good work for education's sake.

—Lakia M. Scott

Introduction

In 2014, the *Washington Post* reported that for the first time, ethnic and racial minorities are the majority student population in U.S. public schools (Strauss, 2014). As American schools increase in diversity, it is imperative that the literacy practices used to teach young students of color reflect the nation's changing demographics. National reports over the past two decades illustrate that the literacy levels of African American and Hispanic/Latino(a) students are continually lower than their white counterparts (Hemphill & Vanneman, 2010; National Center for Educational Statistics [NCES], 2009; 2011).

A National Assessment of Academic Progress Report (NAEP) (NCES, 2015) revealed that only 18 percent of African American fourth graders were proficient in reading. And while NAEP data confirms that there has been significant progress over the last few years for Hispanic students in the elementary grades, language diversity issues remain a major impediment for nonnative English speakers (and their families).

Some recognize these academic performance ratings as a racial achievement gap that exists between black and white students, as well as between Hispanic and white student groups. However, ample evidence supports the notion of an existing treatment gap between these ethnic groups (Cohen, Garcia, Apfel, & Master, 2006; Ladson-Billings, 2006; Lareau, 2003; Milner, 2012).

Consequently, black and brown students either fall victim to highly publicized failure statistics, or they resist recognizing the gains of attaining an education. This assumption is supported through a review of research demonstrating that African American and Hispanic/Latino(a) students are continually overrepresented in school suspensions and school expulsions (Dillon, 2010; Goodman & Hilton, 2010). As a result, there is a need to deeply explore the relationships among black and brown student academic achievement and educational policy, teacher education programs, curriculum, and assessment. Sadly, the educational, social, and cultural needs of traditionally marginalized students are not being met in some public schools.

Fortunately, literacy instruction and research on culturally relevant pedagogy has taken center stage in the form of increased preparation at the teacher education level. Indeed, over the last few years, there has been an uprising of courses and program specializations that seek to inform preservice teachers on culturally relevant pedagogy and instruction. This is also the case in understanding the correlation between urban education and the content areas, especially literacy. The increased attention on examining issues in urban education, with special focus on literacy, is for good reason.

Teaching Literacy in Urban Schools was developed as an attempt to provide novice and experienced educators the practical approaches and interventions for teaching literacy. This book offers a unique perspective on teaching literacy by highlighting the importance of culturally relevant and affirming teaching practices at the elementary, middle, and secondary levels. Through research-based practices and experiential knowledge gained from the field, the authors in this volume are able to capture and chronicle successful approaches to teaching literacy. Unlike other texts that are either directly aligned with theory *or* practice, *Teaching Literacy in Urban Schools* attempts to bridge the two competing perspectives of scholar and practitioner, and instead allow each to have a reciprocal impact on the other. It is our hope that this book will serve as a guide and workbook for educators who seek to engage, inspire, and empower students through the love of learning and literacy.

The first section of the book is intended to provide the reader with an overview of pedagogical approaches designed to meet the literacy needs of middle and secondary urban students. Specifically, the academic, social, and cultural needs that influence adolescent literacy development are presented. In chapter 1, Meredith Dana and Lakia M. Scott review Gloria Ladson-Billings's 1994 book, *The Dreamkeepers*, as part of a research project intended to increase one preservice teacher's knowledge about teaching in urban school environments. Interviewing local elementary literacy educators resulted in findings congruent with the seminal text, and provide implications specific to the literacy cognate.

In chapter 2, Lakia M. Scott and Randy Wood report on a study examining the ways in which elementary preservice teachers enrolled in a reading methods course developed literacy strategies for sixth-grade struggling readers. Findings from the study reveal that 80.2 percent of middle school students increase their fluency development. Additional findings indicate the ways in which elementary preservice teacher developed literacy strategies for their students despite their overall hesitancy and anxiety about the project.

In chapter 3, Lauren Bagwell, Karon LeCompte, and Brooke Blevins discuss spoken word poetry as a tool that can be used to engage students in culturally affirming writing practices. Specifically, the authors define spoken word poetry and discuss its role in the multicultural classroom. They then explain the steps to writing and performing spoken word poetry, and provide three lesson plans that incorporate spoken word poetry into classroom writing practices.

In chapter 4, Mona Choucair focuses on the importance of resurrecting stories through young adult multicultural literature, graphic novels, and digital media in the secondary school classroom. The author discusses the importance of pairing young adult literature with canonized work, and provides a pairing list of texts that have proven successful in English classes. Finally, she describes the role of graphic novels and digital media in promoting close, careful readings of text and comprehension.

The second section of the book focuses on strategies, approaches, and models for increasing literacy motivation and achievement in elementary classrooms. In chapter 5, Amanda Gardner and Evan Ditmore discuss the importance of using aesthetic approaches in teaching writing to counter the regimented forms of process writing. Additionally, this approach helps to empower students by utilizing their voice and background experiences in responding to writing.

In chapter 6, Nancy Gallavan and Gloria Loring report on a descriptive study in which they examined how the 3CO Approach to Writing Instruction, implemented within an urban third-grade classroom, influenced students' writing attitudes and writing performance. Findings suggest that the 3CO Approach positively impacted students' writing motivation and achievement, as well as the teacher's efficacy for teaching writing.

In chapter 7, Margaret Thomson provides foundational concepts for teaching emergent literacy to learners from diverse backgrounds. Interestingly, her discussion on specific approaches to literacy can be especially helpful to upper-grade-level struggling readers.

In chapter 8, Jacqueline Easley describes the illustrator's use of visual elements in Christian Robinson's illustrations for *Last Stop on Market Street*. After discussing the need for beginning readers to actively engage in both the written and visual text of a picture book, she walks the readers through an analysis of how the text's visual elements were used as tools by the illustrator to convey emotions, information, and cultural experiences. The chapter concludes with social justice activities teachers could use with *Last Stop on Market Street*, along with a list of other culturally responsive picture books.

REFERENCES

Cohen, G. L., Garcia, J., Apfel, N., & Master, A. (2006). Reducing the racial achievement gap: A social-psychological intervention. *Science, 313*(5791), 1307–10.

Dillon, S. (2010). Racial disparity in school suspensions. *New York Times*, September 14. Retrieved from http://www.nytimes.com/2010/09/14/education/14suspend.html?emc=eta1

Goodman, G. S., & Hilton, A. A. (2010). Urban dropouts: Why persist? In Steinburg, S. R. (Ed.), *19 urban questions*, pp. 55–67. New York: Peter Lang.

Hemphill, F. C., & Vanneman, A. (2010). Achievement gaps: How Hispanic and white students in public schools perform in mathematics and reading on the National Assessment of Educational Progress (NCES 2011-459). Washington, DC: National Center for Education Statistics, Institute of Education Sciences, U.S. Department of Education.

Ladson-Billings, G. (1994). *The dreamkeepers: Successful teachers of African American children.* San Francisco: Jossey-Bass.

———. (2006). From the achievement gap to the education debt: Understanding achievement in U.S. schools. *Educational Researcher, 35*(7), 3–12.

Lareau, A. (2003). *Unequal childhoods: Class, race, and family life.* Berkeley: University of California Press.

Milner, H. R. (2012). Beyond a test score: Explaining opportunity gaps in educational practice. *Journal of Black Studies, 43*(6), 693–718.

National Center of Education Statistics (NCES), U.S. Department of Education (2009). National Assessment of Educational Progress (NAEP), 1999 trends in academic progress and 2004 and 2008 long-term trend reading assessments. Retrieved from the Long-Term Trend NAEP Data Explorer, http://nces.ed.gov/nationsreportcard/naepdata/

———. (2011). National Assessment of Educational Progress (NAEP), Selected years 1992–2009 reading assessments. Retrieved from the Long-Term Trend NAEP Data Explorer, http://nces.ed.gov/nationsreportcard/naepdata/

———. (2015). National Assessment of Educational Progress (NAEP) 1990–2015 reading assessments. Institute of Education Sciences, National Center for Education Statistics, various years.

Strauss, V. (2014). For first time, minority students expected to be majority in U.S. public schools this fall. *Washington Post-*, August 21. Retrieved from http://www.washingtonpost.com/blogs/answer-sheet/wp/2014/08/21/for-first-timeminority-students-expected-to-be-majority-in-u-s-public-schools-this-fall/

Part I

The Classroom as Community: Academic, Social, and Cultural Needs for Urban Learners

Chapter One

Still Keeping the Dream

Lessons Learned from Successful Literacy Educators

Meredith Dana and Lakia M. Scott

Public school teachers in urban spaces are always challenged with the task of providing culturally relevant and affirming pedagogy to meet the ever-changing instructional needs of their student demographic. Race/ethnicity, socioeconomic class, language, religion, migrant culture, parental situation, and community stability and involvement are among the factors that impact the ways students in urban spaces learn. Notable urban education scholar Gloria Ladson-Billings, in her national bestseller, *Dreamkeepers: Successful Teachers of African American Children* (1994), provided insights to education systems in which teachers contributed to the academic outcomes of students from varied walks of life by holding high expectations for students, empathizing with societal conditions, and providing student-centered instruction.

In light of the continued national trends of academic achievement for students from socially and culturally diverse backgrounds, these insights are still relevant more than two decades later. This chapter will first revisit *Dreamkeepers* by capturing some of the prominent themes of the text. Next, the methodological aspects of this study will be shared, followed by a presentation and discussion of the findings that give credence to the study. Final thoughts will pose recommendations for teaching literacy in urban settings.

REVISITING *DREAMKEEPERS*

Dreamkeepers was written during a time when much attention was given to the achievement ratings of African American students, partly as a reaction to the perspective that this demographic needed separate schooling to meet

3

academic standards. In fact, this question emerges in the first chapter of the text as a possible solution for addressing the statistics on school dropout, expulsions, and other social and economic struggles of students of color.

Ladson-Billings (1994) attempted to capture, as she notes, a "snapshot" of eight experienced educators of African American children. Through her depiction of their teaching experiences and personal interviews, coupled with supporting research and her own personal and professional experiences in education, *Dreamkeepers* is a working guide for understanding, implementing, and continuing culturally relevant teaching practices as a means to provide successful longitudinal outcomes for African American students.

Ladson-Billings capitalizes on the notion that the classroom is a community, and its social structure and inherent culture should work toward a common goal. That is, the way in which knowledge is communicated should be a model in which "knowledge is re-created, recycled, and shared by teachers and students alike" (1994, p. 25). The discourse of learning should have a reciprocal effect, in which the student-teacher dynamic is one that is ever-changing.

The text suggests that this model is not commonly infused in teacher education and preservice programs. Even where there are regimens for curricular and instructional practices that emphasize diversity, these approaches are an assimilationist model that can be seen as a means to generalize instruction, as opposed to appreciating and demonstrating the uniqueness and relevancy of distinct cultural groups.

Additionally, Ladson-Billings (1994) provides a clear indication of why educational reform is vital: "The primary aim of culturally relevant teaching is to assist in the development of a 'relevant black personality' that allows African American students to choose academic excellence yet still identify with African and American culture" (p. 17).

Dreamkeepers provides an opportunity for educators to examine their perspectives on *why* and *how* they teach African American students. In addition, the text challenges teachers to become change agents in recognizing that the social structure of public school systems has already answered her opening query—that there is indeed a "separate-ness" for African American students that perpetuates their educational failures.

EXAMINING SUCCESSFUL PRACTICES FOR TEACHING STUDENTS OF COLOR

Ladson-Billings's (1994) depiction of identifiable traits of African American students, not as "culturally deprived," "deviant," or "deficient" children, but as knowledge shapers whose perspectives are valued within their learning environments, is compelling. The author provides anecdotes from students who interrogate and challenge textbook knowledge, provide comparisons and distinctions from their communities, and conceptualize how some modes of teaching have stagnated their intellectual abilities.

Secondly, the text indicates the importance of understanding one's perspective about African American students. Ladson-Billings (1994) references "dysconsciousness" as an implication for educators who claim to "not see color" in the classroom. In theory, she asserts that this type of teacher is negligent or incapable of developing instruction or curriculum to meet the needs of students of color. Reasons include inherent guilt for the students' ancestral pasts, anxiety about referencing racial and cultural differences, or failure to challenge why a deficit model approach is a norm for this student demographic.

This concept relates heavily to another text by Rains (1998) that discusses the disconnectedness white Americans experience from other cultural groups when attempting to ignore apparent differences associated with white privilege. In understanding how social class struggles and perceptions can preface behavior toward African American students, Ladson-Billings exposes this cultural dilemma. She also relates comparisons among assimilationists approaches versus culturally relevant approaches, as noted in tables addressing self-impressions, social relations, and conceptions of knowledge. In doing so, she provides clear and direct approaches for educators.

Third, Ladson-Billings provides models for reflection, reshaping, and rethinking how educators should approach the teaching of African American students. For example, in *Dreamkeepers* (1994) she provides interpretations of behaviors toward students, including the idea of the teacher as a conductor or coach. Applied, the teacher assumes responsibility and seeks excellence for their students. Additionally, she encourages a greater respect for the experiences and added knowledge a student brings to the classroom, especially if cultural (social, economic, linguistic) differences exist.

And perhaps the author's most vital, yet understated concept for educators is the element of parental involvement as both a necessity and a variable in helping to attain student success. It is essential that teachers are cognizant of the type of familial structures that exist in their schools and surrounding community; harnessing blame on parents without thoroughly deconstructing socioeconomic factors further perpetuates assimilationist models of teaching. Educators should instead look to parents as a resource and avenue for a better understanding of how to facilitate student success.

Finally, dedicated chapters highlight strategies for culturally relevant literacy and numeracy. These suggestions utilize student experiences and build from that knowledge base as well as make the lessons meaningful, intentional, and a forum for expression. Demonstrating that students have the competency to perform academic tasks and are valued in their perspectives are crucial points that this text provides.

Ladson-Billings (1994) helps us understand how culturally relevant pedagogy can mediate oppression and empower students to examine real-world issues from a global sociopolitical consciousness perspective. She encourages teaching students that they have a role to play in making the world a more equitable place; for example, having classroom discussions about the Middle East situation and Vietnam War, in light of disproportionate African American representation in the military, or conducting lessons on Nelson Mandela and South Africa's relationship to African American civil rights.

Ladson-Billings provides in-depth, classroom-based instructional wisdom for improving outcomes for African American students. She advocates for the diversity of staffing, a welcoming environment, adequate grouping in lieu of academic and vocational tracking, adopting cultural language and communication skills, and understanding ways of relating to students and their families, as well as the content, tools, and methods used in the classroom.

The text presents useful insight on improving student outcomes in U.S. urban public schools. The work of Ladson-Billings lends further understanding of the impacts of educating blacks under a white-dominated system as she considers the notion from W. E. B. DuBois (Anderson, 1988) that blacks should perhaps have separate but equal education. Her detailed accounts of successful, culturally responsive pedagogies form recipes of sorts for educators in public schools where African American student outcomes are below grade level due to culturally inappropriate educational strategies.

Ladson-Billings's work is particularly instructive for teachers working directly with children in the classroom. Her approach to culturally responsive teaching is relevant to improving student outcomes in urban schools in the United States, where there exists an achievement gap for minority children when outcomes are measured via standardized testing. Her methods offer hope for narrowing the gap by demonstrating how to address unique learning characteristics of diverse groups of students.

She also points out the frustrations of educators who practice culturally responsive teaching, yet are confronted with opposition by proponents of standardized student accountability. Thus, her work also serves as a voice for these educators, and a call to colleges of education to more adequately prepare all education-related personnel for improving outcomes in diverse urban public school settings.

IDENTIFYING MODERN-DAY *DREAMKEEPERS*: AN ELEMENTARY LITERACY–FOCUSED APPROACH

Inspired by this seminal work, an action research project was developed to allow a preservice teacher the opportunity to engage with local "dreamkeepers" who specialize in elementary literacy. In this study, one education junior (student researcher) was selected to participate in a university grant–funded research project that examined literacy practices of successful educators working in elementary grade schools with a high concentration of students from culturally and linguistically diverse backgrounds.

However, this study differs from Ladson-Billings's (1994) original methodological approach because the focus is not solely on African American learners from a densely populated city. Instead, this study is premised in examining modern-day dreamkeepers who teach a racially diverse student population in more remote but populated areas that have urban-site characteristics (Milner, 2012).

To prepare for the study, preliminary research was conducted in eight school districts in the Central Texas region. Five elementary schools from two school districts were identified for exemplary ratings in English Language Arts and Reading using state and district reports on benchmarks and assessments, student demographics, and overall school characteristics as criteria. From the data provided, school administrators were contacted to solicit information on teachers who would be eligible to participate in the study.

Teachers were considered eligible if they had taught concurrently at the same school and grade for the previous three years, as determined by the administrator (the number of years taught served as a screening variable). From the solicitation requests, eleven teachers were recruited to participate in the study. However, only seven teachers were interviewed for the study. Each teacher participated in an individually structured interview conducted by the student researcher in order to examine (1) how teaching in urban settings differed from other educational environments, (2) what considerations were given to curriculum and instruction practices when working with students from diverse backgrounds, (3) what factors helped students to succeed in reading, and (4) how educators created culturally affirming environments for students.

After the seven interviews were completed, the student researcher transcribed the interview data and conferred with the primary researcher to develop codes, categories, and themes to elicit the significant findings of the study. This study aimed to extend the conversation on culturally relevant teaching with regard to elementary literacy instruction while also highlighting in-service teachers' narratives as a professional development technique for a preservice educator.

TEACHER PARTICIPANTS: AN INTRODUCTION

This section provides a detailed reflection about each teacher participant (pseudonyms were used for participants and the schools in which they taught) through the lens of the undergraduate researcher. Though this study was intended to investigate literacy practices of successful elementary educators, it also served as a professional development opportunity for the student researcher. As such, it is important to contextualize the student researcher's thoughts about each educator. In her words:

> Each of the teacher participants graciously participated, despite their demanding schedules. As I walked into each of their classrooms, the teachers' love for students was evident. The participants had a broad range of experiences and backgrounds which added depth to the study. While race was not a factor in selecting participants, as a white female educator wanting to work in urban schools, it was affirming for me to speak with successful teachers with my same demographic background.
>
> Many of the participants disclosed the sheltered and safe environments they grew up in, and how their students' lives are much different from their own. Still, they rose to the challenge of culturally affirming their students with diverse backgrounds and dedicated themselves to making each student feel important.

Dreamkeeper 1: Amanda

Amanda was a vibrant and passionate veteran teacher with fourteen years of teaching experience in urban schools. She spoke about how much she enjoys the urban school environment and the diverse challenges that teaching in such an environment entails. Amanda taught three blocks of fourth-grade writing with diverse classrooms, and was selected for her success in bringing her bilingual students up to grade level because she taught an entire block of bilingual students who were from Mexico and Puerto Rico.

About half of her students were on grade level, and 20 percent of the total are English language learners. Amanda is a cheerful and determined individual. Despite the pressure she felt to get her students on grade level, it was clear that she did not let that pressure detract from her passion for students. She celebrated every happy moment she witnessed, and reminded herself of the potential for progress daily.

Dreamkeeper 2: Brittany

One of the selected teacher-participants was longtime teaching veteran Brittany, who had twenty-three years of teaching experience. Throughout the interview with Brittany, it was evident how much she values the teaching profession and inspires outsiders to do the same. As a preservice educator who experienced belittling comments about my aspirations to be a teacher, it was refreshing to interact with such a high-achieving and intelligent individual, and it was impressive and inspiring to interview such a highly credentialed individual, who intentionally chose to dedicate her career to students with the highest needs. Brittany's expertise and academic background (she holds a PhD in educational psychology) made her an outstanding urban teacher in her city.

Dreamkeeper 3: Danielle

As a preservice educator conducting these interviews, I became enthralled by teachers who had stayed at the same school for ten years or longer. Danielle was one of the veteran teachers who stood out because she had sixteen years of teaching experience exclusively in urban schools and has taught for eleven years at her current school. She spoke passionately about her students, and shared individual stories about how they have started to come back to her years later as successful high school and college students.

At the time of the interview, 50 percent of her students entered on grade level, and 40 percent of her students were English language learners. Her class was made up of one African American student, two Caucasian students, and nineteen Hispanic students. Danielle inspired me by discussing the diversity of each year, and how she distinctly remembered students and teaching experiences from each year in her career.

Dreamkeeper 4: Jessa

Jessa was a confident yet gentle third-grade teacher at a school where she has taught for three years. It was easy to see why her students loved her and constantly surrounded her, wanting hugs because she took time to make each student in her class feel important. With six years of teaching experience, Jessa remarked on how every year her students come with very different backgrounds, cultures, and ability levels. Since the researchers identified teachers using data from the 2014–2015 school year, Jessa revealed that for that particular school year she looped with her class and taught them for third and fourth grade.

She remarked that she loved teaching students for more than one year, and wishes that she could always stay with her students for two grade levels. Jessa mentioned that her class went from 30 percent of her students on grade level at the beginning of the year, to 100 percent on grade level by the end of their third-grade year. Before this interview, I did not know that teachers could have such a success rate because I had heard so many stories of students being pushed through the system or repeating grades. It became apparent that the success stories of urban educators were not being shared widely, and that preservice teachers needed to know that progress in urban environments is possible.

Dreamkeeper 5: Hillary

Hillary's description of teaching in urban schools was similar to that of the other participants; she said it was both challenging and rewarding. She spoke with certainty about her experiences, and it was clear that her twelve years of teaching English language arts and social studies have given her the necessary experience to be successful. Hillary's class was less racially diverse compared to the other teachers, but she noted that social class differences and cultural differences influenced her teaching practices. Also, Hillary had been known for her ability to integrate content areas to help students become critical thinkers. In fact, she was a leader on her campus for creating engaging curriculum units and resources for beginning teachers.

Dreamkeeper 6: Kelsey

I met with Kelsey in the hallway of her school during her planning period, and although she had a full classroom of third and fourth graders, she offered undivided attention during our interview. Kelsey was organized, and her description of her class revealed that she is very structured and routine-oriented. It became clear that she was able to meet during her planning period because she was already so prepared for the week's lessons. Kelsey was another senior teacher with twenty-five years of teaching experience in urban schools.

She taught a class of twenty third- and fourth-grade students. While she teaches a diverse group of students, she did not have any English language learners in her classroom, which was quite different from her previous years of teaching. Kelsey provided insight into the vast differences between schools categorized as urban schools. She has experience teaching at a school that she considered being "more urban," as she defined that school as having more students that were "more economically disadvantaged and predominantly minorities."

Dreamkeeper 7: Rebecca

When I interviewed Rebecca, who was a graduate of the same teacher education program I am in, she gushed about her love for teaching and was thrilled to share her experiences with me. She teaches the gifted and talented class of fourth-grade students at her school. She claims that 90 percent of her students entered her classroom on grade level, and noted that this is atypically high compared to her other years of teaching at this school.

Her class was made up of ten African American, eight Hispanic, and four Caucasian students. Rebecca is a young, exuberant, and passionate teacher who is outstanding at motivating her students to excel in reading and writing.

FINDINGS AND DISCUSSION

This section details the major themes created through analysis of the interview data collected from the seven teacher participants. These conclusions are directly related to the major topics discussed in *Dreamkeepers*, therefore providing further depth into Ladson-Billings's (1994) theoretical framework of culturally relevant teaching practices. Also, contemporary literature on teaching in diverse settings provided layering for the study's findings.

Desire to Serve

The overall attitude of each of these teachers is positive and caring, demonstrating a major theme, which is the desire to teach and a view of teaching as an act of service. The participants in this study demonstrated a unique desire to serve urban students. These teachers have primarily taught only in urban schools, and repeatedly commented that this had been their only teaching experience. They regard their teaching experiences in these schools as being positive and did not demonstrate any negativity toward the challenges of their jobs.

Each of the participants reflected on the challenges of teaching in urban environments. However, they maintained a positive attitude and viewed their work as highly rewarding. Through the interview process, the participants' compassion for the challenges their students face became apparent. These teachers emphasized the difficulties of their students' home life and individual situations with students. Some reflected on how impressed they are by what students are facing, and how brave the students must be to try to function in a school setting even though they have stressful home lives.

The desire to serve contributes to the teachers' success because they focus on the small ways they help each child, and seem not to be burdened by producing high student outcomes. The desire to serve provides a greater perspective and propels the teacher participants to help students grow in all areas and overcome personal obstacles and hardships.

The way the teachers described their students and teaching showed how committed they are to serving the students by affirming them and providing them support in the classroom that they may not receive at home. They view their job as so much more than meeting state and district standards, and serve their students by providing them with enriching, caring, culturally affirming educational experiences.

Caring Attitude

Out of the desire these teachers have to serve urban students comes their desire to understand their students and build individual relationships with them. The participants strived to create a safe learning environment in which students share their own experiences, which opened the door for teachers to provide further support for students and gain insight into their home life.

Goldenberg (2013) discusses the necessary cultural accommodations for behavior and interaction styles, and how this can play a role in students' engagement and motivation in the classroom. In the study, he addresses the theoretical implications of exchanges between teachers within the dominant culture and students within nondominant cultures. He also posits practical actions teachers can take to address students' culture, which impacts the self-esteem and academic success of students while emphasizing the importance of teachers engaging in critical self-reflection of their own culture and race.

Essentially, teachers must recognize that they are part of a dominant culture and their actions reflect their culture, just as their students' actions are a reflection of culture and upbringing as well. One of the teacher participants, Danielle, provided an excellent example of this caring teaching style that includes cultural accommodations. She allows students to share their own experiences during instructional time, which builds a platform for her to affirm individual students' culture and connect content to what is meaningful for each.

Six of the seven participants recommended that teachers who work with urban students must get to know them and understand where they are coming from, and how to best serve them through teaching. Their view of teaching is not limited to producing high student outcomes, but in helping students grow, learn, and move above and beyond whatever personal obstacles they may face.

One way in which Jessa demonstrated care and her commitment to getting to know her students was the daily question time that she employs. By inviting students to ask her anything they are curious about, Jessa shows that she cares about the students' interests. Jessa does not require that these questions be related to content, so students naturally bring in their own experiences and culture when asking questions.

Question-and-answer segments allow Jessa to affirm culture and build a foundation of student interest and cultural awareness that she can tap into when planning her lessons (Goldenberg, 2013). These real-life questions may illuminate what problems or challenges students are facing, elicit cultural values, and provide the teacher with an opportunity to creatively incorporate the students' culture and interests into future lessons.

Part of the caring attitude these teachers have is demonstrated in their positive view of students. Five of the participants shared that while students do face challenges, they all have the same desire to learn and to be cared for and respected. "Students are the same at heart," and "all children can learn and flourish," were sentiments some of the participants expressed. While students living in poverty do have additional challenges, these teachers stayed true to their belief that children are capable and that they are deserving of love, care, and respect. This positive attitude contributes to their commitment to helping each child, and they are not discouraged that students' circumstances will inhibit them from being successful.

Affirmation

The teachers' caring attitudes—specifically, their commitment to affirming students' success—guided their interactions with students. The teachers believed that students have a need to be loved and cared for, and aimed to celebrate and affirm the students' success. Rebecca demonstrated the high level of acceptance and affirmation in her classroom that is similar to findings in a study on culturally relevant caring. Through a review of current research, Parsons (2005) defines caring as a process of engrossment, receptivity, and reciprocity, and provides vignettes of one teacher, Angel, and her success in putting culturally relevant caring into practice in her classroom.

Caregivers demonstrate empathy, and are dedicated to acting in the best interest of their care recipients. Caregivers act in ways that they would want to be treated as they immerse themselves in the reality of the care recipient and attempt to act in ways that produce the best outcomes. Caregivers accept the care recipients' identities and realities as their own, and this is when caring becomes *culturally relevant* caring. Also, this form of caring provokes reciprocity. In the classroom, that means that students demonstrate caring and act in ways that the caregiver, or teacher, desires.

Similarly, Rebecca recognizes when students are giving their best effort, and publicly affirms and celebrates her students' success. She described that when students write a paper without using nonacademic language, she will raise her voice, clap, and start celebrating and praising them in front of the class. Rebecca's students participate in celebrating one another's learning and achievements. She teaches her students that "academic a-has" are moments when students finally understand something that they have been working on for a long time. When these moments occur in her classroom, her students cheerfully yell "academic a-ha!" and announce to the class what they have learned. Together they all clap and cheer for one another, which is a group demonstration that mimics the caregiver's caring.

Another way that the teachers created an environment affirming to students was by leveling the playing field and identifying that all students, despite their reading abilities, had appropriately leveled assignments. Brittany, like Angel from the Parsons (2005) study, sets high expectations for her students. She highlights the successes of struggling students and continually challenges them to read at higher levels. Additionally, she mentioned that the students set their own individual reading goals, which she supports through monitoring and guided reading activities.

Parent Understanding

An aspect of caring for these students is caring for their families. Goldenberg (2013) addresses some of the false assumptions of low-income families and that some educators have about children living in poverty. Vernon-Feagans, Hammer, Miccio, and Manlove (2001) emphasized the importance of teachers recognizing that students from African American and Hispanic cultures have different literacy experiences at home, but that does not necessarily make them deficient. The teachers in this study demonstrated that they were committed to talking to students and finding out what help they may receive at home regarding literacy and other homework.

Through getting to know students and parents, three of the teachers discussed how their perceptions and attitudes toward parents of urban students changed from a cynical to a caring view. Amanda and Rebecca and Hillary noted that some parents have multiple jobs and simply do not have the time to help students with homework. Or, parents may have had a negative school experience or lack the skills needed to be able to help students. One participant commented:

> I had to change my mindset about the reason for the lack of support and involvement. In the beginning, I thought the parents didn't care. I have come to understand that it is not a lack of concern, but more like a lack of time or know-how. The parents of my students work hard (sometimes two or more jobs). This leaves little time for homework. Also, when parents are uneducated themselves or had a bad school experience, they just don't know how to help.

Instead of growing frustrated by these factors or viewing this as a lack of care for the child's education, these teachers have compassionate and caring attitudes, and they work to overcome obstacles by providing students with adequate instruction in the classroom and the tools they need to help themselves at home.

An often-repeated phrase that these teachers shared was that each student should be treated individually, and their circumstances must be understood and viewed from a caring perspective, knowing that students cannot help their home situations. Rebecca demonstrated how getting to know her students and their circumstances helped her to treat them in a caring way.

Other participants mentioned the difficulty of getting parents involved at schoolwide events, especially if they are working multiple jobs. Amanda suggested creating opportunities that are worthwhile and engaging for parents, that also incentivize their attendance and participation. Amanda's desire to provide parent training aligns with the research suggesting that teachers learn the home literacy practices of their students, and also provide training for parents to help children at home (Vernon-Feagans et al., 2001).

Investing in Cultural Capital

As previously mentioned, the teachers emphasized sharing in their classrooms and inviting students to bring their personal experiences into the classroom. Experience sharing is a culturally affirming practice that allows teachers to start discussions about differences and to respect, value, and celebrate all walks of life that students experience. Creating caring and open environments have led to students from nondominant cultures opening up and sharing examples from their native language during the study of vocabulary.

This case confirms Goldenberg's (2001) finding that allowing students to exchange information and experiences about aspects of their culture fosters positive learning environments and affirms students' cultural capital. Recognizing cultural capital in nondominant cultures and affirming it in the classroom enables teachers to better connect with students and establish positive learning environments. The three practical steps that Goldenberg (2001) recommends are (1) engaging in teacher self-reflection, (2) recognizing the diverse set of students' nondominant culture as valuable within students' contexts and not as a resistance to learning, and (3) embracing cultural capital to engage students in the classroom.

Another helpful strategy was identified by Rebecca, who shares how she seeks to bring in shared experiences for all of her students. Rebecca's class is very diverse and includes some students who have hardly any experiences outside of the central Texas area, and others who have traveled overseas to various countries. She affirms students' culture and emphasizes the experiences that all students can relate to by giving examples or sharing from her own experience. She describes how going to eat at Chick-fil-A is a special treat, and tells stories about the time she went to Walmart or a local skate park. She gets excited about the stories students tell that may seem familiar or less exciting in comparison to the more lavish experiences other students may have had. Again, these teachers' actions are demonstrating their dedication to affirming urban students' cultural capital, and relating content to what is important in their culture and experiences.

The main way that participants affirmed students' culture was through sharing experiences and incorporating multicultural literature whenever possible. Another interesting theme was discovered regarding pedagogy and practice. Two of the teacher participants discussed how they incorporate body movements and hand signs when they teach. For example, these hand signs may be used when students make connections to literature, need help clarifying information, or are summarizing information after reading. This is a culturally affirming practice, because it allows the English language learners and students who struggle to learn to demonstrate their knowledge and understanding to the whole class.

Self-Reflection

One of the questions on the survey protocol allowed for the teachers to reflect on how their perspective on urban education has changed over time. The responses to this question demonstrate how the teachers have engaged in self-reflection and have allowed their teaching experience to shape their perspective over time. One of the teacher participants, Amanda, affirmed that her teacher education program provided her with teaching expertise in an urban school that was vastly different from the school experience to which she was accustomed. The literature reviewed discussed how teachers from the dominant culture tend not to recognize their own culture or reflect on how their upbringing impacts their cultural identity (Goldenberg, 2013).

However, Amanda was able to teach in an urban school as a preservice educator, which forced her to engage in self-reflection about her school experiences. Being in a classroom with so many different cultures showed her the importance of incorporating multicultural literature in her class. The research stated that self-reflection and recognizing one's own cultural identity is not enough on its own, but that teachers must use this self-reflection to prompt culturally affirming behaviors.

FINAL THOUGHTS

Through focusing on teacher narratives and the current stories of success in urban literacy education, the study aligned with the seminal work of Ladson-Billings (1994) *and* more recent literature on teaching in culturally relevant and affirming ways. This particular experience helped to shape one preservice teacher's perspective on teaching in urban environments. The undergraduate student research added this sentiment:

> This project was incredibly insightful to engage in as a preservice educator. While I have had experience teaching in urban schools, the ability to hear from so many teachers about their challenges and what makes them successful was inspiring. When I was a student teacher, I had support and guidance from my mentor teacher, but most of my time meeting with her pertained to getting help on lesson plans or what I needed to do to prepare for the next week. I think it would be extremely beneficial for preservice educators to conduct a research project like this on a smaller scale.
>
> There is so much wisdom that can be learned from these conversations if preservice educators took the time to think of thoughtful and intentional questions that they could ask their mentor teachers that would help bridge the gap for areas that they are not experiencing themselves. In my experience, student teachers are so overwhelmed with the practical aspects of teaching that these conversations are not prioritized and do not happen. Ultimately, the project empowered me to see beyond the challenges and statistical realities of urban

schools, and reinvigorated me to dedicate my career to improving lives of others through education.

In conclusion, the work of Ladson-Billings (1994) continues to be a foundational study that also serves a guide for those who teach in urban environments. As proven through this study, its methodological features can be mirrored in other geographical locales to better understand how to teach diverse learners. Findings from this study also reveal the dire need to revisit curriculum and structures of teacher education models to ensure that such opportunities for novice educators exist.

In the case of the undergraduate researcher involved in this project, the opportunity to engage and interact with successful elementary literacy educators helped to shape perspectives about working in urban schools and reiterate the importance of culturally affirming teaching practices. Indeed, the lessons learned from *Dreamkeepers* (both then and now) continue to breathe life into the work of novice educators and those inspired to serve in urban schools.

REFERENCES

Anderson, J. (1988). *The education of blacks in the south, 1860–1935.* Chapel Hill: University of North Carolina Press.

Goldenberg, B. M. (2013). White teachers in urban classrooms: Embracing non-white students' cultural capital for better teaching and learning. *Urban Education, 49*(1), 111–14. doi:10.1177/0042085912472510

Goldenberg, C. (2001). Making schools work for low-income families in the 21st century. In S. B. Neuman & D. K. Dickinson (Eds.), *Handbook of early literacy research* (pp. 211–31). New York: Guilford Press.

Ladson-Billings, G. (1994). *The dreamkeepers: Successful teachers of African American children.* San Francisco: Jossey-Bass.

Milner, H. R. (2012). But what is urban education? *Urban Education, 47*(3), 556–61. doi:10.1177/0042085912447516

Parsons, Eileen (2005). From caring as a relation to culturally relevant caring: A white teacher's bridge to black students. *Equity & Excellence in Education, 38*(1), 25–34. doi:10.1080/10665680390907884

Rains, F. V. (1998). Is the benign really harmless? Deconstructing some "benign" manifestations of operationalized white privilege. In J. L. Kincheloe, S. R. Steinburg, N. M. Rodriguez, & R. E. Chennault (Eds.), *White reign: Deploying whiteness in America* (pp. 77–102). New York: St. Martin's Press.

Vernon-Feagans, L., Hammer, C. S., Miccio, A., & Manlove, E. (2001). Early language and literacy skills in low-income African American and Hispanic children. In S. B. Neuman & D. K. Dickinson (eds.), *Handbook of early literacy research* (pp. 192–210). New York: Guildford Press.

Chapter Two

Not So Elementary

Preservice Teachers Reflect on Teaching Urban Middle School Struggling Readers

Lakia M. Scott and Randy Wood

Public school education in the United States is an ever-changing landscape that is all too often determined by the political and social climate of the nation. During a time when high-stakes testing measures and teacher accountability ratings determine the overall effectiveness of the school and its leaders, the stakes are also high for those entering the teaching field. For novice teachers, having the necessary skills and experience to handle the daily demands of teaching is proving to be increasingly difficult.

As such, it is imperative for teacher training programs to prepare preservice educators through high-quality academic coursework and deeply enriching field experiences. This chapter will begin with a briefing on the teacher education program at Baylor University and an examination of the Professional Development School model.

An exploration of the elementary Literacy Block follows, and will give further insights into the program as well as provide a rationale for considering a literacy field experience at an *urban school*. Then, a description of the course and the Urban Literacy Project is provided. Findings from the study reveal ways in which elementary preservice teachers developed literacy strategies for sixth-grade struggling readers despite overall hesitancy and anxiety about the project.

BAYLOR UNIVERSITY'S SCHOOL OF EDUCATION TEACHER EDUCATION PROGRAM

The mission of Baylor University's School of Education (BUSOE) is to prepare, within a Christian environment, individuals who improve society through leadership, teaching, research, and service in their professions and communities. As articulated through the Conceptual Framework, the School of Education provides students with varied professional understandings that include planning, development and communication, clinical/field experiences, and assessment of knowledge and skills through diverse learning contexts.

Being ranked among the nation's top twenty education schools located at private universities (*U.S. News & World Report*, 2017), the BUSOE teacher preparation model provides intensified clinical training that prepares leaders to impact the world and shape the future. The Department of Curriculum and Instruction is largely responsible for the undergraduate program and implements a Professional Development School (PDS) model. BUSOE holds national distinctions for establishing strategic and meaningful PDS partnerships with several local school districts that serve students in the greater Waco, Texas, area. At all levels of K–12 schooling, undergraduates receive educational opportunities to work with students from varied backgrounds and communities.

Each semester and calendar year, Baylor students are placed at designated campuses to learn instructional and pedagogical approaches for teaching in the content areas. There are approximately 450 students enrolled in the undergraduate teacher education program, but the vast majority of these students are housed in the elementary certificate program where they are working to become EC-6 generalists.

This chapter will highlight an experimental study with elementary certificate candidates who embarked on a field experience at a public middle school to learn ways to teach literacy, and to develop an increased awareness about working with students from socially, linguistically, and racially diverse populations.

But first, a glimpse inside the tenets of the elementary certification program is needed. Students participate in a rigorous program that provides at least three years of field experiences in school settings (all located on PDS campuses). During the first two years, in addition to taking general education coursework, students work one-on-one with elementary students to learn how to plan lessons and assess academic progress.

Termed "Teaching Associates" during their junior year, students partake in teacher education coursework while also participating in a small-group, instruction-oriented field experience with a clinical instructor. Most notable for the program's intensity during the junior year, Teaching Associates spend approximately twenty hours per week in elementary schools while also taking a full course load of fifteen to eighteen hours. At the conclusion of their coursework and field experiences, Teaching Associates take the state certification exams. Upon passing, these students embark on the final leg of the teacher education journey: a year-long internship.

During the intern year (or two concurrent semesters), preservice teacher candidates attend weekly seminars on issues, topics, and trends influencing teacher education, and spend nine weeks of full-time, whole-class instruction under a mentor teacher. It should come as no surprise that the program's state certification and licensure passage rates are 100 percent since the 2013–2014 school year, and previous years were steady at 99 percent (Baylor University, n.d.).

It is evident that preservice teachers enrolled in the teacher education program garner extensive field experience through the Professional Development School model. However, some would argue that preservice teachers graduate without having varied experiences working with children from culturally, racially, linguistically, and socioeconomically diverse backgrounds, because only a few of the PDS campuses are representative of all of these components.

Interestingly, the teacher education program largely mirrors that of the nation's current teaching force, where 82 percent of elementary and secondary educators in public schools are white, middle-class, monolingual females (U.S. Department of Education, 2016).

However, the nation's demographic of public school students is becoming increasingly diverse—less than half are white, and projections note continually decreasing numbers, while the non-white student population grows larger each year (National Center for Education Statistics [NCES], 2016). As such, it is critical to identify opportunities for teaching instructional approaches that are culturally affirming and academically enriching for tomorrow's changing student landscape.

The purpose of this study was threefold: (1) provide Teaching Associates an opportunity to work and serve children whose racial and socioeconomic characteristics differ from their own, (2) identify literacy strategies that boost academic outcomes, and (3) increase preservice teacher confidence and abilities in teaching students from culturally diverse backgrounds. The aims of the study were grounded in the belief that greater exposure to schools that represent diverse student populations would increase awareness and positive perceptions about teaching in urban schools. The next section provides a brief description of the PDS model.

PROFESSIONAL DEVELOPMENT SCHOOLS: MULTITUDINOUS
IMPACTS ON EDUCATION INSTITUTIONS

A professional development schools (PDS) is an innovative institution
formed through partnerships between professional education programs and
P–12 schools. A statement released by the Executive Council and Board of
Directors of the National Association of Professional Development Schools
(NAPDS) explains what it means to be a professional development school:

> PDSs were designed to accomplish a four-fold agenda: preparing future educa-
> tors, providing current educators with ongoing professional development, en-
> couraging joint school–university faculty investigation of education-related
> issues, and promoting the learning of P–12 students. (NAPDS, 2008, p. 1)

The committee developed nine essential guiding principles to indicate
that PDS partnerships bring benefits to students, teacher candidates, teachers,
principals, university faculty, and communities. Mubuuke, Businge, and Mukule (2014) compare this model to that of teaching hospitals, because the
fields of education and medicine require rigorous academic preparation and
clinical training. Both settings provide support for professional learning in a
real-world environment in which practice takes place.

The College of Education at Penn State University (n.d.) also recognizes
the power and impact of professional development schools as a means for
creating school and university partnerships as a catalyst for educational
change and models for teacher education and professional development.
Since its emergence and subsequent popularity since the 1990s, the PDS
movement has grown substantially with over one thousand school-university
partnerships nationwide.

Currently, Baylor holds PDS partnerships with two public school districts, totaling nine campuses across all grade levels. Cesar Chavez Middle
School (CCMS), located in the Waco Independent School District (ISD), was
the PDS site in which this study took place. CCMS was established in 2001
as a neighborhood school, and a year later moved into a new facility in South
Waco.

According to the Texas Education Agency (TEA), the ethnic composition
of the families in the CCMS neighborhood is 79 percent Hispanic, 17 percent
African American, and four percent white (2016). Of the students at CCMS,
91 percent are classified as economically disadvantaged and eligible to receive free and/or reduced lunch, and 21 percent identify as English language
learners (TEA, 2016).

To provide greater context, over 95 percent of the elementary and middle
school students in the area participate in the free and/or reduced lunch program. And of the district's fifteen elementary schools, CCMS is the zoned

middle school for four sites. Regarding assessment ratings, CCMS has been on a gradual upward incline for academic performance. However, reading proficiency is still a major focus of instruction for the school.

From the information provided about CCMS and its student demographic, it doubly fits to identify the school as *urban*. Milner's (2006) definition of urban schools confirm this designation based on population data and the racial and social contexts of schools in the vicinity. Milner also postulates that these schools are the breeding grounds for preservice educators because they provide a realistic glimpse into the perils of public education.

ELEMENTARY LITERACY COURSEWORK AND FIELD EXPERIENCE

During their stint of the program, in their junior year Teaching Associates are required to complete a designated Literacy Block for one semester. The block includes two courses (Elementary Literacy Methods and English Language Arts Methods) and a concurrent Integrated Language Arts and Reading teaching field experience. Before the Literacy Block, students must have taken a prerequisite course (Early Literacy) that addresses oral language development, phonological and phonemic awareness, alphabetic principles, and the beginning stages of literacy development and practice.

In alignment with statewide teacher education competencies, the Literacy Block centers on elementary-grade-level pedagogy and instruction in English Language Arts and Reading. The Elementary Literacy Methods course focuses keenly on upper elementary literacy practices (grades 3–6).

Topics addressed in this course include the following (as guided by the Texas State Board for Educator Certification [TSBEC]): Literacy Development and Practice (Standard IV), Word Analysis and Decoding (Standard V), Reading Fluency (Standard VI), Reading Comprehension (Standard VII), and Assessment and Instruction of Developing Literacy (Standard X) (TSBEC, 2007).

Over the course of two academic semesters, this study involved sixty-eight Teaching Associates who were enrolled in Elementary Literacy Methods courses—thirty-five in the spring and thirty-three in the fall. Since the course was built with an integrated field experience component, Teaching Associates would typically spend their mornings working in elementary school classrooms. However, most of these experiences were in K–3 classrooms because students built on previous skills learned from the Early Literacy course and work through practical applications and writing conventions from the English Language Arts Methods course.

As a result, there were few experiences for implementing upper-grade-level literacy instructional strategies. This was the rationale for a modification to the course that involved a second field experience component at the sixth-grade level. As such, each Teaching Associate spent four weeks conducting a novel study with two sixth-grade students from Cesar Chavez Middle School.

The Urban Literacy Project was a culminating course assignment in which Teaching Associates would work with middle-grade struggling readers and utilize methods discussed in the course. In this case, "struggling reader" was defined as a student who had significant reading areas that needed improvement, as determined by benchmark assessment provided by the district. These middle school students were selected by the school's literacy specialist, and therefore 100 percent of the student population involved in the study were determined to be struggling readers.

Designated during class time, each Teaching Associate was expected to: (1) spend time assessing students' fluency development, (2) identify a young adult novel based on students' interests and reading levels, (3) create and implement interactive lesson plans that centered on comprehension and vocabulary skills, and (4) produce a case study report that detailed the experience. At the end of the semester, Teaching Associates presented their cases and received feedback from peers and the instructor.

Before the start of the assignment, Teaching Associates created an Urban Literacy Action Plan. Before meeting with students, Teaching Associates received an Instructional Planning Report, which included district reading assessment scores, benchmark performance indicators, and literacy domain analysis to pinpoint specific skills needing improvement.

With this information, the Teaching Associate was able to craft lesson plans that would target particular skills for the student to develop while participating in the novel study. There was added intentionality to pairing students based on domain-specific reading abilities, so that the Teaching Associate could construct lessons that would accommodate both learners. For example, if the Instructional Planning Report indicated that both students needed further practice in analyzing arguments and evaluating texts, the Teaching Associate would be able to implement comprehension strategies throughout the lesson aimed at increasing students' abilities to (1) explain how an author uses reasons and evidence to support a claim, (2) identify stated opinions or beliefs that the author wants the reader to accept, or (3) identify misleading statements and explain why they are misleading.

Teaching Associates then taught middle-grade learners using a guided reading format by creating lesson plans that allowed time for shared and independent reading experiences while also teaching a comprehension and vocabulary strategy to develop literacy skills. Table 2.1 illustrates an example of the Urban Literacy Action Plan, a required component of working with Chavez students. This action plan utilizes the Instructional Planning Report and the intended comprehension and vocabulary strategies taught to enhance students' literacy development and skills.

Findings from the Chavez Experience

One significant aspect of the study was to increase students' fluency ratings through interactive and engaging lessons that strengthened students' skills in comprehension and vocabulary. The DIBELS Oral Reading Fluency instrument is a standardized assessment of accuracy and fluency with connected text (University of Oregon, 2017). This instrument was used to score fluency ratings from pre- and post-assessments.

Findings from the study revealed that 80.2 percent of students increased their fluency development (N=91). Also, Teaching Associates noted that while some students did not have increased fluency ratings, there was still demonstrated improvement in the students' ability to comprehend text and answer questions about what was read. Other key aspects of the study were to examine the extent to which the lessons helped students' comprehension and vocabulary skills. There was a notable improvement in these areas as well. However, the remaining findings will focus more on the growth and development of the Teaching Associates.

On Teaching Literacy

Some Teaching Associates shared the ways they approached teaching reading. As highlighted in the excerpts below, most found compatibility with identifying comprehension and vocabulary strategies to build on concepts associated with each of the literacy domains. Students were also able to connect other aspects reading—such as motivation and interest—to increase students' overall engagement throughout the sessions. One example of this is highlighted here:

> I noticed my student struggled most with reading comprehension, and I attributed this to many factors including his lack of interest, lack of internal motivation, and lack of self-confidence with reading. In order to improve his comprehension, I chose texts and passages that would meet his unique learning style, engage him in reading, and encourage him to build self-confidence in his abilities. Additionally, I noticed that my student struggled with his memory retention of vocabulary and lacked necessary skills for decoding words. In formatting appropriate instruction, I ensured that every time my student and I met for tutoring, we reviewed prior knowledge of vocabulary and learned new and unfamiliar vocabulary terms in a variety of ways. In reflecting on his progress, and his improvement from the first tutoring session to the last, I noticed a difference in my student's self-confidence, his application of comprehension strategies, and his vocabulary knowledge.

Table 2.1. Urban Literacy Action Plan

Student: Robyn	**Skill Development Needed in (Domains):**
Reading Level: 4.5	• Comprehension Strategies and Constructing Meaning
Student: Michelle	• Analyzing Literary Text
Reading Level: 4.5	• Understanding Author's Craft
	• Analyzing Argument and Evaluating Text

	Domain Focus	**Planned Readings, Strategies, and Skills**
1	**Pre-assessment**	Students will take the DIBELS pre-fluency assessment and be introduced to the book, *Esperanza Rising*. Begin reading chapter 1.
2	**Analyzing Literary Text**	Students continue reading *Esperanza Rising* (chapters 2–3). While reading, I plan to implement the *Character Four Square* and *Inference Chart* strategies in order for students to develop the following skills: • Identify the narrator in a story or poem told from the first-person point of view. • Describe the setting and analyze how it contributes to the story. • Understand the relationship between a character's actions, traits, and motives and describe the main character's interactions with other characters.
3	**Under-standing Author's Craft**	Students continue reading *Esperanza Rising* (chapters 4–5). While reading, I plan to implement the *Directed Reading-Thinking Activity* and *Sketch to Stretch* strategies in order for students to develop the following skills: • Understand why the author may have chosen to include certain sensory details. • Understand how word choice affects the feeling or mood of a text. • Understand the meaning of words and phrases used figuratively.
4	**Compre-hension Strategies and Constructing Meaning**	Students continue reading *Esperanza Rising* (chapters 6–7). While reading, I plan to implement the *Venn Diagram* strategy in order for students to develop the following skills: • Compare and contrast information and conclusions in text on the same topic. • Recognize cause-and-effect relationships by comprehending the meaning of a whole passage rather than by identifying individual cue words. • Use main and supporting details to understand texts.
5	**Compre-hension Strategies and Constructing Meaning**	Students continue reading *Esperanza Rising* (chapters 8–9). While reading, I plan to implement the *Semantic Mapping* strategy in order for students to develop the following skills: • Make and check predictions by using prior knowledge, ideas from text, text features, and obvious foreshadowing clues. • Identify the author's purpose and explain how the reader can determine purpose.

6	**Analyzing Literary Text**	Students continue reading *Esperanza Rising* (chapters 10–11). While reading, I plan to implement the *Character Feelings* and *Connections Chart* strategies in order for students to develop the following skills: • Describe the setting and analyze how it contributes to the story. • Understand the relationship between a character's actions, traits, and motives and describe the main character's interactions with other characters. • Identify how a story's plot is influenced by a character's actions.
7	**Analyzing Argument and Evaluating Text**	Students continue reading *Esperanza Rising* (chapters 12–13). While reading, I plan to implement the *Questioning the Author* strategy in order for students to develop the following skills: • Identify the author's main claim and identify reasons to support the claim. • Identify misleading statements or images by comparing them to facts.
8	**Post-assessment**	DIBELS post-fluency assessment and concluding thoughts on the book, *Esperanza Rising*.

Based on this excerpt, this Teaching Associate was also able to build the student's confidence level in reading, which can have lasting effects on his academic experiences. In the next passage, a Teaching Associate was able to pinpoint a particular strategy that would provide consistency and reiteration of literacy concepts to help students further their reading comprehension. This theme is exemplified below:

> Using my vocabulary and comprehension strategy book, I was able to come up with a few different learning strategies to use with my students that could help improve certain concepts that they otherwise struggled with. I chose the Sketch to Stretch strategy, because I loved the idea of it and I thought it would be something my students would be able to complete successfully. This practice helps them retell a scene from the story that stood out to them, that they remember, or was their favorite. Students chose a scene, sketched it out, and then wrote a little caption or description of what they drew and what was happening in the scene. I knew this was a skill that both students struggled with, so I wanted to try this out and see how they did on it.

The Sketch to Stretch strategy, as developed by Short, Harste, and Burke (1996) offers students a way to the extend meaning and respond to narrative readings through connecting, visualizing, and inferring. Also, this comprehension strategy can be used to help students to become more comfortable in talking and working in small groups on their illustrations. The excerpt above demonstrates the Teaching Associate's ability to identify skills and target intervention while also providing an authentic and enjoyable reading experience for the middle-grade learner.

However, a few Teaching Associates were not as effective in creating literacy lessons to assist in developing struggling reader's abilities. Feelings of anxiety for teaching an upper-grade-level group, and overall unease about the experience of working in an "urban" school, hindered their ability to be open-minded and focused on the task at hand. The following quote exemplifies this theme:

> I feel as though I did not learn much about trying to help students improve on reading because I was not excited about it coming into this experience. I know that I could have done a much better job of coming up with ways to help my students, but I always had so much more going on that I did not give it my all. I thoroughly enjoyed spending time with my students and getting to know them on a personal level far more than the reading aspect of it all. Sadly, I feel that my feelings toward the reading part were more transparent because my students were hardly ever excited about it, as well. I learned more about the strategies I used after writing about them, especially the ones that were presented in class. Most were very interesting and things I would consider using in my future classroom, regardless of the grade level.

Despite not adequately preparing and implementing this project, the Teaching Associate still recognized the potential she could have had on improving the middle-grade learners' outlooks on reading. Ultimately, not giving this experience priority consideration was indeed a missed opportunity, which is unfortunate but not uncommon for some preservice teachers.

Misperceptions reinforce some of the perspectives about teaching upper-grade students in elementary teacher education programs: that primary grade instruction is less difficult and, in the primary grades, the teacher has more support from teachers and parents. However, this is a misconception, and one of the main reasons this additional field experience was needed. Also, in consideration of the coursework, an experience where students can readily utilize teaching and concepts of literacy instruction for upper-grade learners was critical in the preparation of an EC-6 educator certification.

Another concern that may not have been explicitly stated was the notion of teaching in an urban school. As previously discussed, the preservice teacher demographic at Baylor does not match the student populations at the PDS campuses, nor are socioeconomic characteristics congruent.

For preservice teachers, not having a field experience component in a school with highly diverse student populations throughout the duration of a teacher education program would not only be highly detrimental in educator preparation, but also deeply unrealistic in shaping perspective about the current teaching field.

On Teaching Upper-grade-level Learners

Teaching Associates also shared how this experience changed their views about teaching upper-grade-level learners. From the sum of their experiences, Teaching Associates were able to connect the learned instructional strategies to practical applications for struggling readers.

However, most Teaching Associates noted the familiarity of working through literacy concepts with the realization that, despite the difference in age, students needed explicit and direct instruction to enhance their abilities in comprehension and vocabulary. One Teaching Associate mentioned how the experience allowed her to gain more confidence in her teaching. The following quote provides greater elaboration:

> Before this field experience, I was apprehensive about working with upper-grade levels and concerned that my teaching would not have any effect on their reading comprehension and fluency skills. After this field experience, I was confident that I could meet the individual needs of the students by leveling with them and approaching them as a friend and mentor instead of a teacher. In conclusion, this experience has impacted my confidence in working with sixth-grade students and has taught me how to adapt to teaching middle school students in urban school settings.

Here, the Teaching Associate recognized the importance of establishing connections and building relationships when teaching. Her realization is directly connected to Noddings's (2005) notion of the ethic of care, in which an educator deeply considers the ethical and moral foundations of teaching and learning while also examining the relationship between schooling and welfare.

Another finding from the study was that Teaching Associates become realistic about academic expectations for students. One Teaching Associate shared how this opportunity was a worthwhile lesson learned about considering the expectations a teacher has for her students. The following quote exemplifies this theme:

> Rather than setting goals for my student, I allowed [this student] to set his own individual goals, and I kept him accountable for meeting these goals and striving to do his personal best every time we met. I watched him progress at his own pace and it was a beautiful thing, because all progress is good progress.

From this quote, it is also important to realize that teachers are learning to disrupt the "deficit model" approach of lowering academic and personal expectations regarding students. Instead, this Teaching Associate (along with many others) participated in discourse that would allow for authentic learning to occur by situating learning with understanding culture, language, and identity (Dworin & Bomer, 2008).

Finally, this experience encouraged some Teaching Associates to expand their horizons toward teaching upper-grade-level students. The following quote provides greater elaboration:

> This experience encouraged me to be a teacher that pays attention to students' needs, both personal and academic. I was afraid of working with the sixth graders but there was always a small part of me that wanted to teach older students. Once the experience ended, I realized that I enjoyed it a lot more than I thought I would. I definitely plan on going on to get a higher certification later in life.

This experience was valuable for the Teaching Associates because they were able to make connections from the sum of their academic experiences in the Literacy Block—from primary to upper-grade levels. Teaching Associates continuously discussed how they were able to use strategies taught in *all* literacy classes to further their student's academic growth and experiences in reading. And, many mentioned that they were more empathetic to the work demands of teaching literacy in an urban school setting because of the intentionality and care that is required for authentic learning to unfold.

FINAL THOUGHTS

The purpose of this study was to provide Teaching Associates with a field experience that represented greater student diversity as well as improved their and abilities for teaching literacy. An unexpected finding of the study was the increased levels of confidence that Teaching Associates felt as a result of the experience.

And in some cases, Teaching Associates expressed a desire to teach in urban school populations. However, since the start of the Urban Literacy Project, modifications have been made to improve the academic and learning outcomes for those involved. In particular, the format of the project has been adapted to feature literature circles and small-group settings with daily mini-lessons.

In the modified format, the course instructor administers the reading interest inventory to middle-grade students at the start of the semester. An earlier administration of the reading interest inventory gives Teaching Associates more time to compile a list of possible books of interest for middle-grade readers. Thus, more time is also available for Teaching Associates to read the young adult novels in preparation for the experience.

Since Teaching Associates are expected to create and implement lessons specific to literacy strategies, having read the text in advance is beneficial for increasing opportunities for scaffolding instruction. From this compilation, middle-grade students can rank-order books they would like to read. From their responses, small reading groups can be formed among the students and facilitated by two or three Teaching Associates. In the small-group or literature circle format, time can be allotted before and after convening for mini-lesson activities and exercises.

In closing, the Urban Literacy Project has been impactful for both Teaching Associates and middle-grade learners. As mentioned earlier, middle school students gained confidence about their reading, and most improved their reading rates. While this experience cannot be indicative of larger leaps of academic success for middle-grade struggling readers, it can be reasonably concluded that it has some influence on their perceptions and experiences in reading.

Also, some Teaching Associates who initially felt hesitant about working with upper-level students have learned how to be adaptable and push through anxieties for the sake of teaching *and* learning.

REFERENCES

Baylor University. (n.d.). *Outcomes*. Baylor School of Education website. Retrieved from http://www.baylor.edu/soe/index.php?id=935145

College of Education, Penn State University. (n.d.). What is a professional development school? Retrieved from https://ed.psu.edu/pds/elementary/general-information/what-is-a-professional-development-school

Dworin, J., & Bomer, R. (2008). What we all (supposedly) know about the poor: A critical discourse analysis of Ruby Payne's "Framework." *English Education, 40*(2), 101–21. Retrieved from http://www.jstor.org/stable/40173273

Milner, H. R. (2006). Preservice teachers' learning about cultural and racial diversity: Implications for urban education. *Urban Education, 41*(4), 343–75.

Mubuuke, A. G., Businge, F., & Mukule, E. (2014). The intricate relationship between a medical school and a teaching hospital: A case study in Uganda. *Education for Health (Abingdon, England), 27*(3), 249–54. http://doi.org/10.4103/1357-6283.152183

National Association of Professional Development Schools (NAPDS). (2008). *What it means to be a professional development school*. Retrieved from http://napds.org/wp-content/uploads/2014/10/Nine-Essentials.pdf

National Center for Education Statistics. (2016) State nonfiscal survey of public elementary and secondary education, 2004–05 and 2014–15, and National elementary and secondary enrollment by race/ethnicity projection model, 1972 through 2026. Washington, DC: U.S. Department of Education.

Noddings, N. (2005). *The challenge to care in schools: An alternative approach to education* (2nd ed). New York: Teachers College Press.

Short, K. G., Harste, J. C., & Burke, C. (1996). *Creating classrooms for authors and inquirers* (2nd ed.). Portsmouth, NH: Heinemann.

Texas Education Agency. (2016). 2015–16 report card: Cesar Chavez Middle. Retrieved from http://curriculum.wacoisd.org/UserFiles/Servers/Server_11618/File/Accountability/ReportCards/2015-2016/ReportCard-ccms.pdf

Texas State Board for Educator Certification (TSBEC). (2007). English language arts and reading generalist EC-6 standards. Retrieved from http://tea.texas.gov/Texas_Educators/Preparation_and_Continuing_Education/Approved_Educator_Standards/

University of Oregon. (2017). *DIBELS oral reading fluency and retell fluency*. Retrieved from https://dibels.uoregon.edu/assessment/dibels/measures/orf.php

U.S. Department of Education. (2016, July). The state of racial diversity in the educator work-force. Retrieved from https://www2.ed.gov/rschstat/eval/highered/racial-diversity/state-racial-diversity-workforce.pdf

U.S. News & World Report. (2017). *Best elementary teacher education programs*. Retrieved from https://www.usnews.com/best-graduate-schools/top-education-schools/teacher-education-rankings

Chapter Three

Writing with Spoken Word Poetry

The Power of the Pen in Classrooms

Lauren Bagwell, Karon LeCompte, and Brooke Blevins

Democracy needs her poets, in all their diversity, precisely because our hope for survival is in recognizing the reality of one another's lives.
—Bill Moyers

Students comprise the citizens that will determine the future of democracy. If teachers are going to teach affirming writing practices in the classroom, they must first recognize that they have a voice. There is a need for curriculum to teach students how to communicate their ideas, and more importantly, how to listen to the perspectives of others. Helping students to develop and use their voice begins by creating a culturally affirming environment in which multiple perspectives are not only included, but expected *and* respected in the classroom as part of the everyday curriculum. Spoken word poetry is a tool that can be used to engage students in culturally affirming writing practices while also engaging each student's voice.

Spoken word poetry has the power to promote dialogue around current events and social issues, and help students establish connections. Spoken word poetry provides hopeful pedagogical possibilities for engaging students in culturally affirming writing practices that lead to greater understandings of themselves, one another, the social studies content, and their role as active citizens. This chapter explains in detail what spoken word poetry is, the role of spoken word poetry in the multicultural classroom, and implications for elementary and middle school classrooms. In addition, lesson plans that incorporate spoken word poetry into classroom writing practices are provided.

WHAT IS SPOKEN WORD POETRY?

Spoken word poetry is a type of poetry that relies on the art of storytelling and wordplay while also having strong ties to the hip-hop culture (Parmar & Bain, 2007). "Spoken word is written on a page but performed for an audience. It relies on a heavy use of rhythm, improvisation, rhymes, wordplay, and slang" (Power Poetry, n.d.). Poetry provides students with a medium through which they can express themselves and construct meaning out of their reality, acting as a viable outlet for communicating the obstacles presented by social realities experienced by youth (Fisher, 2005; Jocson, 2005).

American poetry is currently enjoying revitalization in the public realm. Less than twenty years ago, poetry was declared "dead" to the public because it was largely practiced within the academy, but poetry events can now command mainstream and even commercial audiences, and enjoys popularity with youth (Somers-Willett, 2006).

In the classroom, poetry can help cultivate a safe space for elementary and middle school students to "talk back to injustice" as they discuss and process social issues they are experiencing in their everyday lives (Christensen & Watson, 2015). Spoken word poetry allows students to talk about current events in the classroom, provide their insight, and explore and affirm the perspectives of their classmates. As students interact with the art form, they can identify generative themes within the curriculum and engage in both a local and global conversation that draws from their lived experiences (Desai & Marsh, 2005).

WHAT DOES SPOKEN WORD POETRY MEAN FOR THE MULTICULTURAL CLASSROOM?

Through poetry, we can mourn our losses, expel our terror, tell our stories, and sing our joys.
—Christensen and Watson, *Rhythm and Resistance*

Culturally relevant teaching is a pedagogy of opposition, committed to both individual as well as collective empowerment (Ladson-Billings, 19954). It serves as a way for educators to acknowledge the experiential knowledge and culture of students and integrate students' lived experiences, values, and understandings into the classroom curriculum (Brown-Jeffy & Cooper, 2011). Gloria Ladson-Billings (1995b) argues that culturally relevant teachers allow students to maintain their cultural integrity, teach students to be culturally competent, have a critical consciousness, and make connections to their everyday lives. Furthermore, having a culturally relevant classroom environment is essential to helping students develop cultural competence about social justice and equality. In short, culturally relevant pedagogy is a call to counter exclusionary narratives by becoming culturally aware of teaching practices and learning environments.

Spoken word poetry can help to provide a safe space to engage multiple perspectives. Bolton and Latham (2004) suggests that writing poetry allows "memories, thoughts, and reflections on experience to be explored and expressed" (p. 120). By allowing alternative perspectives and text-to-self connections to enter the classroom, the teacher is creating space for meaningful relationships between teacher and student to take place.

Spoken word poetry allows students to engage in democratic learning and connect what they are learning in their classroom to their own lived experiences. Jocson (2005) found, in case study research conducted in two multicultural high school classrooms, that spoken word poetry can bridge school and out-of-school literacy practices of young people, and in turn make the material relevant and engaging to students. Spoken word poetry as an art form is an affirming process for students because poetry allows teachers and students to see education as a social process (Kinloch, 2005).

Infusing spoken word poetry into elementary and middle school classrooms can provide students with a space to link the knowledge and practices of social studies with an understanding and appreciation of their culture, as well as the culture of their classmates. Vardell (2003) suggests that poetry can be used within the curriculum to introduce a new topic, to supplement content, or to expand on thematic ideas.

In accordance with Christensen & Watson (2015), spoken word can assist middle school educators in cultivating a culture of conscience by creating a safe space for students to discuss and process current events and social issues in their everyday lives. By incorporating spoken word poetry into the classroom, teachers can create a learning environment that permits both complex and subtle forms of thinking and reflection to take place (Eisner, 2002). Additionally, Darts (2004) argues that poetic expression can be used as a tool to encourage students to participate in important public conversations regarding the social and political relations of art to power, culture, and democratic citizenship.

TEACHING WHAT MATTERS THROUGH POETRY

The National Council of Teachers of English (NCTE) argues:

> During this era of high-stakes testing, technology-based instruction, and increased control over students' expression due to school violence, students' right to write must be protected. Censorship of writing not only stifles student voices but also denies students significant opportunities to grow as both writers and thinkers. Through the process of writing, students develop strategies to help them come to understand lessons within the curriculum as well as how

their language and ideas can be used to communicate, influence, reflect, explain, analyze, and create (NCTE, 2014)

The purpose of writing in the classroom has undergone a change from traditional stances to those that encompass technological resources. Students write for many reasons: developing social networks; reasoning with others to improve society; engaging in personal and spiritual growth; reflecting on experience; communicating professionally and academically; building relationships with others, including friends, family, and like-minded individuals; and engaging in aesthetic experiences.

Students can and should write about what matters to them. This process of writing requires a new approach to teaching writing. In this approach, teachers should look to incorporate high-quality writing instruction into the classroom daily, in a way that is culturally relevant to the learner. This process can be achieved by applying the following writing instruction guidelines established by Graham et al. (2012) to lessons that utilize spoken word poetry as a pedagogical tool. These scholars suggest that writing is a means to allow students to communicate what matters to them and help them connect with others.

Graham et al. (2012) recommend that teachers:

- Provide daily time for students to write
- Teach students the writing process
- Teach students to write for a variety of purposes
- Teach students to become fluent in handwriting, spelling, sentence structure, and writing with a computer
- Create an engaged community of writers

These guidelines can help teachers establish a positive and encouraging environment for writing. Spoken word poetry is a writing practice that can be utilized to teach students about the writing process, as well as how to write for a unique purpose. In addition, spoken word poetry's focus on performance is a powerful way to engage communities of writers, while helping students connect with others. As an overall term, "performance poetry" can encompass a number of different types of verse in performance: slam poetry, avant-garde performance poetry, hip-hop, and song lyrics. Here the term "spoken word poetry" denotes a subset of performance poetry (Somers-Willett, 2006). Audiences are almost exclusively using the term to indicate a hip-hop infused lyric and, in many cases, spoken word poetry is indistinguishable from hip-hop (Sommer-Willet, 2006). Ladson-Billings reflects on the process of using spoken word poetry in the classroom. She states that classroom teachers need:

A fresher version of culturally relevant pedagogy that meets the needs of this century's students. In developing this theory, culturally sustaining pedagogy use culturally relevant pedagogy as the place where the "beat drops" and then layer the multiple ways that this notion of pedagogy shifts, changes, adapts, recycles, and recreates instructional spaces to ensure that consistently marginalized students are repositioned into a place of normativity—that is, that they become subjects in the instructional process, not mere objects. (Ladson-Billings, 2014, p. 76).

Arguing that hip-hop should be viewed as a culture rather than a strategy in a lesson plan, Alim (2011) challenged education researchers to not only look at the literacy skills that can be taught using this medium, but also at how young people can acquire other skills, such as those for civic participation (Fisher, 2005).

WRITING AND PERFORMING A SPOKEN WORD PIECE

There are numerous possibilities and benefits for students using spoken word poetry. Students can conduct research, take a stand, and speak out about topics and issues that are personally significant. These range from discrimination and corruption, to rare birds on the endangered species list. Students can also explore how figurative devices gleaned from English courses can be applied to a form of writing that students enjoy. Students begin to not only play along with different literary devices, but also with how taking on a different perspective can better tell the story. How does the story of the Civil War change when it's told through the perspective of a tree at Gettysburg? Or a musket?

Spoken word poetry can be used for self-expression and reflection. Importantly, students can see how writing can be utilized for healing and other personally meaningful purposes. It is a safe space for students to explore their emotions about losing a loved one, having an absent parent, or feeling the pressure of making good grades. It is a place where students can reflect on the day they made the basketball team or on a mentor that changed their lives. Poetry is affirming because there is room for all emotions.

The following lessons demonstrate that through the writing and performance of spoken word poetry, young people can experience the relevance of poetry, learn more about important issues, stand up for what they believe in, and see poetry in the world around them (Williams, 2015).

Steps to Writing and Performing Spoken Word Poetry

Power Poetry (n.d.) outlines five steps to writing and performing a spoken word piece:

1. Do your homework.
2. Choose your topic.
3. Put your words on paper.
4. Edit your draft.
5. Add a little drama.

Have Students Do Their Homework

Before writing a spoken word piece, it is important that students become familiar with what spoken word poetry is. The more exposure students can get watching others perform, the better. Have students check out local coffee shops or bookstores that offer any open-mic events or poetry slams. If all else fails, YouTube is a great resource! A few popular resource channels on YouTube are *Write About Now, Button Poetry*, and *Def Jam*.

Choose a Topic

Have students consider the following: Is there a person who has changed your life? Is there an event that has significantly changed you for the better or for the worse? Are there any injustices you have witnessed firsthand? These are all gateway questions for students to begin writing their first spoken word piece (Power Poetry, n.d).

Put Words on Paper

Start with a few sentences and encourage students to take risks and to welcome mistakes. Some of their best ideas will come when they just let the words flow out of their pen. Power Poetry suggests that the best place to start is with the five senses. As students think about their topic, have them consider what they see, hear, taste, touch, or smell. The more senses poets can incorporate into their poem, the more vivid the story or picture is painted for the audience. The more details students can include about their topic, the better. Advise students to let their words flow into a "natural rhythm," and then organize their lines into stanzas. Remember, not all poetry has to rhyme (Power Poetry, n.d).

Edit the Rough Drafts

Power Poetry (n.d.) states that the best way to edit a poem is to read it aloud. When a student reads a piece aloud, it helps them better decipher any lines that are lengthy or awkward. Students may also find that some lines might be better suited elsewhere in the poem.

Add a Little Drama

The goal of spoken word poetry is to create a performance piece. Think of ways that can invoke the emotions of the audience. What lines need to be read softer or slower? Are there any parts of the poem that should be read faster, louder, or even shouted? How can one's body language be used to better tell the story? Something to note for your students: there are no props allowed in slam. Therefore, it would be in the teacher's best interest to discourage students from using props.

In any classroom, there may be students who love to write or who may be thinking, "I'm not gifted or creative enough to write a piece." The good news is that spoken word poetry has no particular format. Students can write in paragraphs or write in stanzas. The point is that spoken word poetry is a user-friendly medium.

LESSON PLANS INCORPORATING SPOKEN WORD POETRY INTO THE CLASSROOM

Boxes 3.1 and 3.2 present lesson plans with ideas about how to get students started.

BOX 3.1. CULTURE AND IDENTITY ACTIVITY

Activity 1: 4th–8th Grade

Theme: Culture and Identity
Goal: Students will be able to explain how authors use literary devices, figurative language, and stylistic elements to create meaning; reflect on a historical and cultural setting of a literary work; and create their piece of literary work about their lived experiences.

Introductory Writing Prompt:

Think about how your family, friends, enemies, and mentors have impacted your identity. Discuss with the class how our culture and relationships within and outside that culture may impact our identity.
Have students share their responses to the writing prompt.

Analyzing Poems:

Poem 1: Read this excerpt from Lauren Bagwell's "Where I'm From."

I'm from cowboy boots and horse riding stereotypes. Lake houses on a hot July day and snow that falls once every other year. I'm from small town suburbia where everyone knows your business.

I'm from scrunchies, Beanie Babies, Polly Pockets, Raggedy Ann and Andy, and LEGO. I'm from trying to see the screen of my Game Boy Color in the dark in hope of conquering Ash and Pikachu's goal of finally catching them all.

I'm from a childhood where I didn't just have an imaginary friend but an imaginary neighborhood. My back yard transformed into a crime-fighting super hero world with a swing set as home base and a sand box full of possibilities.

I'm from watching the sun set most days from a soccer field, wearing a #6 jersey under the lights. Running up and down the sideline looking for the perfect cross. Hoping a striker finishes it off into the net. Knowing when it does, the perfect sound will signal the perfect ending.

Thinking about the poem: After reading this piece as a class, have students read the poem on their own, circling words they don't understand and underlining images they enjoy. As students complete reading the poem on their own, come back as a class and discuss any confusing or challenging words. What have we learned about the author through this poem? What did you enjoy about this piece? What did you dislike? What images stuck out?

Poem 2: Watch this video of Georgia Lyon's poem "Where I'm From." https://www.youtube.com/watch?v=ZdnHl_yW1dQ

Comparing the poems: Have students answer the following questions:

> How are these poems similar? How are they different?
> How do both authors use the concept of "showing and not telling"?
> In what ways do you relate to where each author is from?

Writing your poem: Students will write their own "Where I'm From" poem following our project outline. Students will finish by reading their poems aloud to the class.

Discussion Questions:

> What is something new I learned about my classmates?
> Were there any classmates that you shared similar lived experiences with?
> Whose poem surprised you the most?
> How has your culture defined who you are as an individual?

Closure:

Finish the lesson with having your students watch this video representation of the Human Family by Maya Angelou: https://www.youtube.com/watch?v=fyzI2Lu9Qcw. Angelou writes, "We are more alike my friends than we are unalike."

BOX 3.2. WHERE I'M FROM PROJECT

For this project you will create both a poem and a visual.

Directions for the Poem

You will create a poem based on the "Where I'm From" poems we have read in class. You will use the poems by Georgia Lyon and Natalie Wright as your examples. Your poems **must include at least 10 stanzas** and **no more than 15 stanzas**. These stanzas can be written in any order that you want and can be in any format that you want. You do not have to begin each stanza with "Where I'm From . . ." but you can if you want to.

You must include the following:

1. **One stanza describing the environment of where you're from.**
   For example: *I'm from small town America—woods and farms and barbeques, two lane highways and no lane rivers, a land of no subways, no buses, no Starbucks.*
2. **One stanza describing the things you played with as a child.**
   For example: *I'm from a childhood climbing trees, jumping into rivers, playing with Ninja Turtles.*
3. **One stanza describing the trends of your *era*.**
   For example: *I'm from Osh-Kosh and B-gosh, the Jetsons, ponytails and scrunchies, New Kids on the Block, and all those other embarrassing 80s moments.*
4. **One stanza describing the type of music you listened to.**
   For example: *I'm from music—the piano, the harmonica, the clarinet. Baritone, trumpet, guitar. I sing with the Beatles, Billy Joel, Bonnie Raitt, and Crosby, Stills, and Nash.*
5. **One stanza describing the type of books you read.**

For example: *I'm from the Boxcar Children, Amelia Bedelia, the Hardy Boys, Encyclopedia Brown, Nate the Great, the Baby-sitters Club.*

6. **One stanza describing the trends of the type of shows you watched.**

    For example: *I'm from Get Smart, Cheers, M*A*S*H, Taxi, Saturday Night Live.*

7. **One stanza describing the phrases or expressions you may have heard in your everyday life.**

    For example: *I'm from the know-it-alls and the pass-it-ons, from Perk up! and Pipe down! I'm from He restoreth my soul.*

8. **One stanza describing your individual style.**

    For example: *I'm from jeans and flip-flops, surfboards and skateboards, CCD and Pre-K, family and friends, fog delays and snow days.*

9. **One stanza describing your family and culture.**

10. **One stanza about anything else you want to tell your audience.**

Directions for the Visual

You will need to create a visual to go along with your poem. Your visual should include images, words, or symbols that illustrate what your poem is describing. This visual can be a painting, a collage of pictures, a cartoon, word art, a landscape drawing, a model, or any other visual you can think of. **This must be done on a separate sheet of paper.**

The lesson presented in Box 3.3 focuses on haiku, which are easy to write and provide an ideal format for student expression.

BOX 3.3. HAIKUS FOR GRATITUDE ACTIVITY

Activity 2: 6th–8th Grade

Theme: Writing Haikus for Gratitude
Goal: Students will be able to analyze a series of haikus and discuss their meaning. Students will be able to explain what gratitude is, and why it is important. Students will be able to write their haikus for gratitude.

Introductory Writing Prompt

Have students begin by watching The Science of Happiness video, "An Experiment in Gratitude": https://www.youtube.com/watch?v=oHv6vTKD6lg
Then have students respond to the following prompt: Write about a time you've been truly grateful.

What is a Haiku?

Haiku is a Japanese form of poetry that challenges poets to convey a vivid message in only seventeen syllables with a structural format of five–seven–five. In this format, the first line has five syllables, the second line has seven syllables, and the third line has five syllables. Have students watch Zezan Tam's TED Talk, "The Power of Daily Haiku": https://www.youtube.com/watch?v=O72QqfwYwho&t=787s

Students will read a series of haiku poems by poet Daniel Garcia (2017).

Poem 1: Thanksgiving

> Vending machine says,
> "Thank you. Have a nice day." I
> say, "Thank you. You too."

Poem 2: Sunlight

> They ask me what I'm
> grateful for. I say sunlight.
> Not because it brings
>
> light into the world,
> or that it's the source of all
> life, but rather, I
>
> say sunlight because
> sunlight always gives me some-
> thing to stretch towards

Comparing the Poems

How does the author display gratitude in each of these poems? How are these poems similar or different?

Writing your poem: Students will practice writing their haiku poems for gratitude. What are you thankful for? Extra guacamole on your burrito? Something in nature? A friend or family member? Remember the five–seven–five format! Have students share their haikus with the class.

Discussion Questions:

> What are the different things we are thankful for?
> How does showing gratitude make a positive impact on who we are as individuals?
> In your opinion, how does the haiku format impact the audience differently than other forms of poetry?

Closure:

Have students write a haiku for gratitude to one person they are thankful for. Have them give that haiku to that person.

The lesson plan outlined in Box 3.4 requires students to compare objects. Comparing objects offers students the opportunity to examine various perspectives.

BOX 3.4. VOICE AND PERSONIFICATION ACTIVITY

Activity 3: 6th–8th Grades

Theme: Love Poems Between Inanimate Objects
Goal: Students will be able to analyze the voice and personification in different examples of spoken word poetry. Students will be able to explain how personification is used to enhance a poet's piece of writing.

What Is Personification?

Personification is the projection of human characteristics onto inanimate objects, deities, or forces of nature. These words can be verbs or adjectives that are typically only used to describe the human condition. Personification is also used to project emotions and motives onto objects incapable of having human thoughts or feelings (Personification Examples and Definition, 2015). In poetry, we see personification as a valuable tool that allows the writer to bring creativity and introduce alternative perspectives into their writing through the use of figurative language. The following activity looks at the use of personification and alternative perspectives in different spoken word pieces.

Introductory Writing Prompt

Students will begin by making a list of different inanimate objects. Have your students make a list of at least twenty different inanimate objects. These can be things they see in the classroom, things they have in their room, or things they see on the street or at the park. When students are finished writing, have them read through their list and choose two objects. They can only pick two. Have students keep this list out on their desk. We will come back to this list later in the lesson.

Analyzing Poems

After creating their lists, have students watch Sarah Kay's poem entitled "Love Letter from the Toothbrush to the Bicycle Tire" as performed at the Urbana Poetry Slam in November 2010. The class will then watch a student example of a similar type of poem entitled "Love Letter from Milk to Freezer." After viewing, have students discuss the similarities and differences between the two poems.

Video 1: https://www.youtube.com/watch?v=BIAQENsqcuM
Video 2: https://www.youtube.com/watch?v=mQQCtdG1WDU

Discussion Questions

How do these poems use personification to tell a story?
Why do you think these poets chose to personify these specific objects?
In your opinion, in what ways does personification add or take away from the poem?
How does personification alter your perspective about the relationships between different objects?

Writing Your Poem

It is now time for the students to return to the lists they created earlier in their warmup. The idea is that your students stick with the two objects they originally circled. For their writing assignment, students will create a poem in which they write a love letter between the two objects they circled earlier. When students are finished, have them share with the class.

Reflection

What two objects did you write about?
How did you choose to personify these two objects?
How did using personification alter your perspective on how you
   thought about these two objects?

Each of these lessons provides examples of how to engage young people with poetry as an art form. These lessons certainly can be modified to fit the needs of individual students.

FINAL THOUGHTS

This chapter provided a detailed description of spoken word poetry, examined the role spoken word poetry plays in a multicultural classroom, described the implications for the elementary and middle school classroom, and provided lesson plans that incorporate spoken word poetry into classroom writing practices.

In writing spoken word poetry, students can make sense of their lived experiences. This writing practice can empower students to deal with difficult issues, and can provide ways for them to express their feelings authentically to audiences in safe spaces. Use of these lesson plans can help students and teachers see how writing can be utilized for healing and other personally meaningful purposes. Through the writing and performance of spoken word poetry, young people can experience the relevance of poetry, learn more about important issues, stand up for what they believe in, and see poetry in the world around them (Williams, 2015).

Culture typically functions as a double-edged sword in schools. As Ladson-Billings (2014) has argued, teachers who are not aware of their students' culture display a level of ignorance that leads them to make suppositions about those students and cite low self-esteem as the cause of students' academic and disciplinary problems. On the other hand, teachers who understand their students and recognize the importance of their students' culture and interests are likely to create a genuine learning community in which students are actively engaged. Spoken word is familiar to progressive teachers who recognize that introducing this form of poetry can change their students' views on literature, as well as their relationship to it (Fiore, 2015). Ladson-Billings developed a program for her students entitled, "First Wave," and she describes how she engages her students by teaching the history of hip-hop poetry using alternative texts—hip-hop lyrics, videos of hip-hop artists, and close readings of and 1960s-era protest poetry, and thus notices that students were regularly collaborating outside of class to develop and practice their spoken word poems (Ladson-Billings, 2014).

Spoken word poetry promotes an appreciation of diversity. It also allows students to access writing in personally meaningful formats. The genre of spoken word poetry promotes democratic ideals and practices by helping students explore and communicate current issues in their respective communities and beyond. Through poetry, students learn that they have a voice. Recognizing that their voices matter is a beautiful lesson for students to learn.

REFERENCES

Alim, H. S. (2011). Global ill-literacies: hip hop cultures, youth identities, and the politics of literacy. *Review of Research in Education, 35*(1), pp. 120–46.

Bolton, G., & Latham, J. (2004). "Every poem breaks a silence that had to be overcome": The therapeutic role of poetry writing. In G. Bolton, S. Howlett, C. Lago, & J. K. Wright (Eds.), *Writing cures: An introductory handbook of writing in counseling and psychotherapy,* pp. 106–22. Hove, UK: Brunner-Routledge.

Brown-Jeffy, S., & Cooper, J. E. (2011). Toward a conceptual framework of culturally relevant pedagogy: An overview of the conceptual and theoretical literature. *Teacher Education Quarterly, 38*(1), 65–84.

Bruce, H. E., & Davis, B. D. (2000). Slam: Hip-hop meets poetry—a strategy for violence intervention. *English Journal, 89*(5), 119–27. doi:10.2307/822307

Christensen, L., & Watson, D. (2015). *Rhythm and resistance: Teaching poetry for social justice.* Milwaukee, WI: Rethinking Schools.

CNN Money. (2016). Apple ad spotlights diversity in time for Olympics [Video file]. August 4. Retrieved from https://www.youtube.com/watch?v=fyzI2Lu9Qcw

Colleen Boye (2010). A poem by George Ella Lyon [Video file]. December 11. Retrieved from https://www.youtube.com/watch?v=ZdnHl_yW1dQ

Darts, D. (2004). Visual culture jam: Art, pedagogy, and creative resistance. *Studies in Art Education, 45*(4), 313–27. Retrieved from http://www.jstor.org/stable/1321067

Desai, S. R., & Marsh, T. (2005). Weaving multiple dialects in the classroom discourse: Poetry and spoken word as a critical teaching tool. *Taboo, 9*(2), pp. 70–90.

Eisner, E. W. (2002). *The arts and the creation of mind.* New Haven, CT: Yale University Press. Retrieved from http://www.jstor.org/stable/j.ctt1np7vz

Fiore, M. (2015). Pedagogy for liberation: Spoken word poetry in urban schools. *Urban Education and Society 47,* 813–29.

Fisher, M. T. (2005). From the coffee house to the school house: The promise and potential of spoken word poetry in school contexts. *English Education, 37,* 115–31.

Garcia, D. (2017). Sunlight. Unpublished poem.

Garcia, D. (2017). Thanksgiving. Unpublished poem.

Graham, S., Bollinger, A., Booth Olson, C., D'Aoust, C., MacArthur, C., McCutchen, D., & Olinghouse, N. (2012). Teaching elementary school students to be effective writers: A practice guide (NCEE 2012-4058). Washington, DC: National Center for Education Evaluation and Regional Assistance, Institute of Education Sciences, U.S. Department of Education. Retrieved from http://ies.ed.gov/ncee/wwc/publications_reviews.aspx#pubsearch

Jocson, K. M. (2005). Taking it to the mic: Pedagogy of June Jordan's poetry for the people and partnership with an urban high school. *English Education, 37*(2), 132–48.

Kinloch, V. (2005). Revisiting the promise of "students' right to their own language": Pedagogical strategies. *College Composition and Communication, 57,* 83–113. Retrieved from http://www.jstor.org/stable/30037899

Ladson-Billings, G. (1995a) But that's just good teaching! The case for culturally relevant pedagogy. *Theory into Practice, 34*, 159–65.

———. (1995b). Toward a theory of culturally relevant pedagogy. *American Educational Research Journal, 32*, 465–91.

———. (2014) Culturally Relevant Pedagogy 2.0: a.k.a. the Remix. *Harvard Educational Review, 84*, 74–84.

Lynch, P. (2007). Main content area making meaning many ways: An exploratory look at integrating the arts with classroom curriculum. *Art Education, 60*(4), 33–38.

Lyon, G. E. Where I'm from. *Smithsonian Education*. http://www.smithsonianeducation.org/educators/professional_development/workshops/writing/george_ella_lyon.pdf

Matthews, J. (2016) Am lit spoken word. [Video file]. April 12. Retrieved from https://www.youtube.com/watch?v=mQQCtdG1WDU

National Council of Teachers of English (NCTE). (2014). NCTE beliefs about students' right to write. Retrieved from http://www.ncte.org/positions/statements/students-right-to-write

Parmar, P., & Bain, B. (2007). Spoken word and hip hop: The power of urban art and culture. *Counterpoints, 306*, 131–56.

Personification Examples and Definition. (2015). Retrieved from http://www.literarydevices.com/personification/

Power Poetry. (n.d.). 5 Tips on Spoken Word. Retrieved from http://www.powerpoetry.org/actions/5-tips-spoken-word

Somers-Willett, S.A. (2006). Def poetry's public: Spoken word poetry and the racial politics of going mainstream. *Iowa Journal of Cultural Studies 8/9* (Spring-Fall). Retrieved from https://uiowa.edu/ijcs/def-poetry%E2%80%99s-public-spoken-word-poetry-and-racial-politics-going-mainstream

SoulPancake. (2013). An experiment in gratitude: The science of happiness [Video file]. Retrieved from https://www.youtube.com/watch?v=oHv6vTKD6lg

Speakeasynyc. (2010). Sarah Kay: A love letter . . . [Video file]. February 6. Retrieved from https://www.youtube.com/watch?v=BIAQENsqcuM

TED. (2016). Zezan Tam: The power of daily haiku [Video file]. May 17. Retrieved from https://www.youtube.com/watch?v=O72QqfwYwho&t=787s

Vardell, S. M. (2003). Poetry for social studies. *Social Education,67*(4), 206–11.

Williams, W. R. (2015). Every voice matters: Spoken word poetry in and outside of school. *English Journal, 104*(4), 77–82.

Wright, N. (n.d.). Where I'm From. *Scholastic*. Retrieved from http://teacher.scholastic.com/writeit/PDF/wright.pdf

Chapter Four

Lovin' the Skin I'm In

Resurrecting Stories in the Secondary English Classroom

Mona M. Choucair

Recently, a university professor had a conversation with one of her former preservice candidates who was elated because "she actually got to teach young adult literature" in her new high school teaching position. She shared that her students loved Sharon Flake's *The Skin I'm In* so much that they *actually* read the book cover to cover, passed the unit test, and even started a schoolwide book club, simply because they became so excited about reading.

One might ask, "What got them so excited?" It is the need for stories that are relevant in teenagers' lives—stories that involve characters who look like them, and themes that address the issues that they actually face today. Maleeka, the main character in *The Skin I'm In*, learns to love herself again despite being bullied because of a skin condition. Her story resonates with teenagers who face bullying in schools and in online and social media forms. According to Morocco & Hindin (2002), "In experiencing the rewards of entering Maleeka's world and deliberating about her choices, . . . [students] see how Maleeka takes responsibility for how others see and treat her and they may also reflect more on their own choices and expand their own social identities" (p. 157).

Moreover, this young adult novel proves successful with urban students because it allows a sociological perspective on the text, it displays multiple literacies, it can be taught using student-centered discussions, and it teaches excellent critical-thinking skills (Morocco & Hindin, 2002).

This chapter emphasizes the importance of resurrecting stories through young adult and multicultural literature, graphic novels, and digital media in the secondary school classroom, and the ways that English teachers can

49

increase adolescents' love for reading, improve reading comprehension, and facilitate the writing process.

The author of *The Fault in Our Stars*, John Green, discusses the need for stories in middle and secondary English classrooms. He remembers that children's literature was impactful to him as a boy "because [he] saw [him]self in it" (2014, p. 2). Green contends that authors are always resurrecting storylines, making them their own, and that teachers must allow students to create their own stories. Reading young adult literature fosters that creativity in students.

It is increasingly apparent that secondary English teachers must resurrect the power of stories through young adult literature, graphic novels, and digital media. The more teens read and know, the better readers and writers they will become. This is a paradigm shift of sorts. Kelly Bull (2011) affirmed this idea when she wrote, "[F]acilitating rich literacy opportunities for young adults is essential in order to provide a student-centered approach to reading that teaches young adults how to read, think, make connections, and take action" (p. 229).

YOUNG ADULT (YA) LITERATURE

Young adult literature is "rich and complex," offering students "authentic language and addressing issues that are relevant to contemporary adolescent readers" (Bull, 2011, p. 223). YA literature, such as *The Skin I'm In*, offers a sophisticated reading alternative for students, provides relevant plot lines for adolescents, builds positive attitudes toward reading, and supports comprehension.

Wadham and Ostenson (2013), contend that "young adult literature in the classroom is not only a good tool to help our students build the critical and analytic skills they need, but [also a] body of literature with the greatest likelihood to build positive attitudes toward reading for the maximum number of readers" (p. 18). YA literature provides access and relevance to adolescent readers. "The exploding numbers of young adult titles testifies . . . that teens are hungry for books that speak to them and eager to read when they find the literature personally compelling. . . . A respect for young adult books helps teens to know that their perspective and ideas are valid" (Wadham & Ostenson, 2013, p. 20).

Emig (2015) states that students are more apt to read and understand literature to which they can relate: "Young adult literature show students that there are other people who are struggling with the same thoughts and feelings [that] they are" (p. 6). Gibbons, Dail, & Stallworth (2006) adds that YA literature is a great way to approach complex issues that adolescents often face. Thus, English teachers must select literature that is appropriate and relevant.

Contemporary realistic fiction, the broad category under which most YA titles reside, proves relevant because the narrator's voice is one that teens easily recognize: "Teens respond to young adult literature in part because they can relate to the voice conveyed. Successful young adult literature usually sounds like real teens talking . . . [and] it is the authenticity of these voices that makes for rich complex narratives" (Bond, 2011, p. 253).

In order to "foster a love for reading," students must have some choice in what they read in a secondary English classroom (Emig, 2015, p. 6). Doing so will help them become more engaged and increase their reading comprehension as well. Megan Truax notes that "it is a well-known fact that people enjoy reading texts that interest them" (2010/2011, p. 7), so it should be no different for adolescents. The more these adolescents are allowed to choose what they want to read, the more motivated they will be to read. However, giving students a choice in what to read scares most teachers. Yet, most teachers don't realize that they do not have to read all of these books! They merely have to make them available to the students, either by having them in the room or by suggesting titles.

Multicultural Young Adult Literature

The power of story must be presented through a diverse, multicultural lens. Multicultural literature presents a "powerful medium for understanding the world in which we live . . . [and offers students methods for] develop[ing] new meanings and conceptualizations of what diversity means" (Bond, 2011, p. 30). "People rarely belong to just one culture; we have varying levels of competency in several cultures and especially when we are teens, there is a fluidity of identity as we seek to discover who we are" (p. 34). Diverse stories that appeal to young people present a mirror through which students can see glimpses of themselves.

Palmi, Augsburger, and Havere (2016) stressed the importance of YA novels in the secondary classroom, stating,

> Teachers must think about, value, and develop their understanding of multiculturalism in the classroom . . . [the] most important weapon a teacher has is information; a teacher [must have] some degree of cultural education in the classroom . . . and an understanding of how their pedagogy might be shaped through the design of lessons and management of resources in order to meet the potential needs of their students. (p. 17–18).

The following YA novels promote multicultural awareness:

- *The Skin I'm In* (2000) by Sharon G. Flake. Maleeka, the thirteen-year-old main character, is an African American girl with a rare skin condition that makes her a prime target for teen harassment and bullying. She struggles with low self-confidence and loneliness. The novel won the coveted Coretta Scott King Award for young adult fiction.
- *Esperanza Rising* (2000) by Pam Munoz Ryan. Esperanza, the young main character in this epic novel, tries to learn her place in life as a major life experience turns her family unit upside down. The novel takes place in Mexico, and addresses family tragedy and reconciliation.
- *Tears of a Tiger* (1994) by Sharon Draper. Andy, the main character of this novel, must struggle with the guilt of killing his friends in a drunk-driving accident. The content of the novel is all too familiar to its teen audience. The attraction of this novel lies in its multimodal format, relying on newspaper accounts, personal stories, and journal entries.
- *The Absolutely True Diary of a Part-time Indian* (2007) by Sherman Alexie. Arnold Spirit, Jr., the main character of this controversial novel, moves from the Spokane Indian Reservation to an all-white public school in Washington. Junior's life is presented in diary form and addresses crushes, sexuality, alcoholism, and other teen issues. The novel is very popular with young male readers.
- *Buried Onions* (1999) by Gary Soto. Eddie, the main character in this often depressing novel, tries unsuccessfully to escape poverty and makes many mistakes along the way. Set in the crime-ridden barrio of Fresno, California, the novel addresses very real effects of poverty in teen life, such as theft, drinking, and depression.
- *Monster* (1999) by Walter Dean Myers. Steve Harmon, the main character in this multilayered novel, proves fascinating to young readers. Steve tells his story from prison through the vehicle of his own screenplay and journal entries. The novel is very personal and has won numerous awards, including the prestigious Michael J. Printz award as well as the Coretta Scott King Award.
- *Habibi* (1997) by Naomi Shihab Nye. The protagonist of this beautiful story, a young woman named Liyana Abboud, must move from St. Louis to Palestine, the native land of her Arab father. This bildungsroman captures the raw emotions of a young girl transplanted in a strange place as she navigates the normal emotions of a teenager and learns about living in two worlds with two identities. The book has won the American Library Association (ALA) Best Young Adult Novel Award and numerous other awards.

Pairing Young Adult Literature with the Canon

English teachers must embrace young adult literature, not as a replacement for the canonized work, but more so as companion pieces. Asking students to make connections between young adult literature and the canon involves them in the learning process, allows them to transfer prior knowledge to a new text, and inspires them to read more.

By integrating contemporary YA literature into their lesson plans and novel units, teachers offer adolescents a rich experience well beyond that of the traditional classroom. Much of the popularity of young adult literature lies in its great diversity, as seen in table 4.1, which shows pairings that have proven very successful in English classrooms.

Young Adult Literature and Technology

Brock, Goatley, Raphael, Trost-Shahata, and Weber (2014) note that English teachers must be aware of the ever-changing technological world in which our students live. Since they are constantly on their iPhones and iPads, students must *re*-learn to interpret text—the actual written word—very carefully, and "as teachers we must make sure that students see their own cultures represented in literature or current issues and topics" (p. 4).

Furthermore, English Language Arts and Reading (ELAR) teachers must ensure that adolescents have access to "age-appropriate materials and complex texts" (Brock et al., 2014, p. 9). By focusing on the power of story—stories like their own—teachers can hook students into a love of reading and foster in them a sense of confidence in discussing literature.

Additionally, if educators will recognize blogs, diary entries, journals, Facebook posts, and tweets as viable YA "texts," then they can build effective, multilayered literature units that students will enjoy. "While not full-length novels, Facebook pages, search result listings, or comment boards that teens peruse certainly count as reading in the sense of decoding and comprehending text," state Wadham and Ostenson (2013, pp. 18–19). After all, the authors continue, "to create independent readers, the environment we create in our classrooms should not only portray how to read at a critical level but also how to engage with reading on a personally pleasurable level as well" (p. 19).

THE GRAPHIC NOVEL

The medium of graphic novels may present the most popular method for hooking teen readers. English teachers may ask, Why the graphic novel? Joy Lawn (2012) responds: "Visuals generally capture attention. . . . Kids love movies and graphic novels have a close relationship with movies. . . . It is

Table 4.1. Pairing YA Literature with Traditional Canon

YA Novel	Traditional Canon
The Fault in Our Stars, John Green	Emily Dickinson's poetry
Sunrise over Fallujah, Walter D. Myers	*The Red Badge of Courage*, Stephen Crane
The Outsiders, S.E. Hinton	"Flowers for Algernon," Daniel Keyes
Postcards from No Man's Land, Aiden Chambers	*The Diary of Anne Frank*, Anne Frank
The Hunger Games (series), Suzanne Collins	"The Most Dangerous Game," Richard Connell "The Lottery," Shirley Jackson
The Book Thief, Markus Zuzsak	*Number the Stars*, Lois Lowry
Speak, Laurie Halse Anderson	*A Thousand Sisters: My Journey into the Worst Place on Earth to Be a Woman*, Lisa Shannon
The Giver, Lois Lowry	"Harrison Bergeron," Kurt Vonnegut
The Secret Life of Bees, Sue Monk Kidd	*Uncle Tom's Cabin*, Harriet Beecher Stowe
Silent to the Bone, E. L. Konigsberg	*Diving Bell and the Butterfly*, Jean-Dominique Bauby
Buried Onions, Gary Soto	*The House on Mango Street*, Sandra Cisneros
Night, Elie Wiesel	*The Boy in the Striped Pajamas*, John Boyne
The Battle of Jericho, Sharon Draper	*The Perks of Being a Wallflower*, Stephen Chbosky
Looking for Alaska, John Green	*A Separate Peace*, John Knowles
The Lightning Thief, Rick Riordan	"Persephone," from Greek mythology
Sold, Patricia McCormick	*The Scarlet Letter*, Nathaniel Hawthorne
Monster, Walter D. Myers	*The Count of Monte Cristo*, Alexandre Dumas
13 Reasons Why, Jay Asher	Slam poetry
Coraline (graphic novel), Neil Gaiman	Edgar Allan Poe's short stories
The Skin I'm In, Sharon Flake	*Their Eyes Were Watching God*, Zora Neale Hurston

helpful to remember that graphic novels use the language of young people—filmic, visual, immediate—capable of handling multiple characters and storylines in a flexible, original way" (p. 30).

Therefore, teachers must accept graphic novels as valid literature. Lawn suggests that "graphic novels are worth investigating . . . because they are enjoyed by students and have many features that are both motivating and able to underpin explicit and worthwhile teaching opportunities" (2012, p. 26). Graphic novels help students learn strategic reading patterns and promote close, careful readings of text. Being adept at visual literacy helps students learn to "decipher and de-code" texts, which are defined as "graphic," meaning "graphics, pictures, illustrations, and comics" (Lawn, 2012, p. 27); thus, graphic novels serve as "natural progression[s] of the picture book, the novel, the art book, [and so forth]" (p. 27).

Moreover, librarians and media specialists alike endorse graphic novels, comics, and magazines. Specifically, the appeal of graphic novels boosts students' willingness to read, transfers power of comprehension back to the adolescent reader, and makes an array of subjects more stimulating. According to Bucher and Hinton (2006), "Contemporary adolescents are growing up in a visual and digital society where the use of pictures to present information is often the norm and where teens are more comfortable with visual styles found in those formats" (p. 278).

Without a doubt, adolescents find visual print media more attractive than the written page. "Graphic novels are a fusion of art and text that builds on the impact of visuals to offer value, variety, and new medium for literacy" (Bucher & Hinton, 2006, p. 287). Many educators use graphic novels to introduce literary terms, to serve as bridges to classic literature, and to scaffold writing assignments. School librarians consider graphic novels essential because of their wide popularity among students, and their reflection of a wide range of genres including fantasy, mystery, geography, history, science, and the classics. "The mere fact that [graphic novels, comics, and magazines] are in a school library or classroom collection give[s] legitimacy to that publication" (Bucher & Hinton, 2006, p. 297).

Along with promoting visual literacy through "reading" and navigating the white/black spaces of the various plates, the graphic novel presents a unique form of storytelling. Alverson (2014) states that graphic novels "reinforce left-to-right sequence like nothing else. The images scaffold . . . [sentences] and [offer] a deeper interpretation of the words and story. The relative speed and immediate enjoyment build great confidence in readers" (p. 3).

Research by Karen Gavigan (2012) suggests that graphic novels increased reading motivation for boys, English language learners, and special needs students, and can help teach multiple literacies (p. 20). Leading reading researchers agree that the very appearance of plates and bubbles helps focus students' attention on the page. And so, "[f]or weak learners and readers, graphic novels' concise text paired with detailed images helps them decode and comprehend the text" (Meryl Jaffe, quoted in Alverson, 2014, p. 3).

Moreover, graphic novels help adolescents write better; after students learn to "read" panels, they should be encouraged to "write out the action of a page or two using descriptive prose . . . which usually demonstrate[s] two things: First, their ideas about what actions connected the images we see in each panel. Second, how effective comics are for communicating information" (Alverson, 2014, p. 4).

An excellent writing assignment stemming from studying graphic novels asks students to create original plates for a graphic novel, complete with dialogue bubbles, narration, and illustration. Therefore, students actually create their own stories and learn to appreciate another art form.

DIGITAL MEDIA

"The reluctant reader [readers who do not like the novels chosen by their teachers or those readers who struggle with reading comprehension] dilemma reaches its peak in middle school. At this time, academics become less important than the many other factors happening in these students' lives," notes Megan Truax (2010/2011, p. 4). In addition to employing YA literature, teachers must embrace digital media to hook teen readers.

Rebecca Hill (2010) also confirms, "Nowadays, young readers are tech savvy. . . . This generation of readers has more distractions than any previous group, thus creating a tectonic shift in how educators must assess and motivate struggling readers. This is where technology and books collide" (p. 9). Multiplatform books fuse traditional print books with entertaining computer applications, making books enjoyable and easily accessible.

Multiplatform books can also cross subject lines, as in the *Mackenzie Blue* series by Tina Wells, which "includes money tips" and could be used as a "jumping off point for mini lessons in economics and ecology" (Hill, 2010, p. 11). Another popular multiplatform tool is FanFiction, "where readers get involved as a reviewer or author," giving students a chance to "develop a sense of story elements online" (Hill, 2010, p. 10–11).

Obviously, the key to attracting teens to the reading process is a modern/ familiar platform that tells an enticing story. Digital media has proven successful in getting reluctant readers to read because it is "a convergence of story and the arts . . . for the purpose of aiding human connection and expression" (Gunter & Kenny, 2008, p. 85). In their article, "Digital Booktalk: Digital Media for Reluctant Readers," Gunter and Kenny note that teachers must use cutting-edge technology to help remove the stigma for poor readers.

Many adolescent students cannot or will not read, simply because "they do not interact well with text based materials" (Gunter & Kenny, 2008, p. 86). In other words, paper materials seem antiquated and unfamiliar, so they do not respond positively to them. Therefore, according to the authors, "the effective use of digital media as a part of an integrated instructional strategy [teaches] reading and writing to otherwise reluctant readers" (p. 86).

One example of how digital media connects to specific literature is Rick Riordan's *The 39 Clues* series. In this multiplatform text, characters Ann and Dan Cahill enter into a "worldwide quest in search of 39 clues. Using history and geography . . . the books include gaming cards that readers can use in their own virtual travels" (Hill, 2010, p. 10).

Another popular example is *The Amanda Project: Invisible I*, by Stella Cennan and Melissa Kantor. This eight-book series focuses on finding mischief-maker Amanda, who pranks high schoolers and then mysteriously disappears. "The website, www.amandaproject.com, provides a zine for readers to upload their own art and writing projects, clues to the mystery, and a chat forum" (Hill, 2010, p. 11).

Gunter and Kenny (2008) affirm that for today's teens, "the preferred first language of the media culture may help [in] overcoming literacy deficiencies" (p. 87). They also recommend movie trailers as part of the pre-reading visualization that "has been shown to increase reading proficiency by providing an organizing structure" (p. 88) for poor readers. After all, teens love images, as evidenced by their love for Instagram, Facebook, and Snapchat; this love for image translates easily to digital media.

Digital Storytelling

Students must create their own stories. That's where digital storytelling comes into play. Fortunately, the tools needed for digital storytelling—computers, scanners, digital cameras, and high-quality digital audio devices—have become increasingly more affordable and accessible (Robin, 2008, p. 222).

Costello and Reigstad (2014) stated that digital storytelling allows teens to use their computers to "become creative storytellers. . . . This material is [then] combined with various types of multimedia, including computer based graphics, recorded audio, and [so forth] (p. 4). Often called "multiliteracy," this approach to writing/storytelling provides students with "opportunities to design multimodal narratives that represent and reflect on their sociocultural identities and their lives" (Angay-Crowder, Choi, & Yi, 2013, p. 38).

Teens obviously take great pride in creating their own stories and images in their real lives, so posting things in the digital sphere comes quite naturally to them. Hence, the best aspect of digital storytelling shows that students actually want to share what they read and what they learned.

The benefits of digital storytelling for educators are numerous: teachers may use these stories to "enhance current lessons within a larger unit, as a way to facilitate further discussion," teach "digital literacy, global literacy, technology literacy, and visual literacy" simultaneously, and teach students to "critique their own work, as well as the work of others, facilitating social learning and emotional intelligence" (Angay-Crowder, Choi, & Yi, 2013).

For further information and examples, educators may visit the University of Houston's "Educational Uses of Digital Storytelling website, located at http://digitalstorytelling.coe.uh.edu/.

FINAL THOUGHTS

John Green made his mark on the literary world through his best-selling young adult novels such as *The Fault in Our Stars* and *Looking for Alaska*. He obviously knows his adolescent audience: "For contemporary kids, who can find sufficient distractions in gaming and video, I think books must do something more" (2014, p. 4). He is correct. By adopting young adult and multicultural literature, graphic novels, digital media, and digital storytelling, English teachers *can* do more. And while he enjoys the many accolades of his literary success, Green remains positive that "we can grow the breadth and diversity of YA literature. We need to get more YA books to kids. . . . And *then* the stories will endure" (2014, pp. 5–6).

YOUNG ADULT LITERATURE CITED

Alexie, S. (2007). *The absolutely true diary of a part-time Indian.* New York: Little Brown and Company.
Anderson, L. H. (1999). *Speak.* Harrisonburg, VA: Donnelley & Sons.
Asher, J. (2007). *13 reasons why.* New York: Penguin.
Chambers, A. (2002). *Postcards from no man's land.* New York: Penguin.
Collins, S. (2008). *The hunger games.* New York: Scholastic Press.
Draper, S. M. (2003). *The battle of Jericho.* New York: Athenaeum Books.
———. (1994). *Tears of a tiger.* New York: Aladdin.
Flake, S. G. (2000). *The skin I'm in.* New York: Hyperion.
Gaiman, N. (2002). *Coraline.* New York: HarperCollins.
Green, J. (2005). *Looking for Alaska.* New York: Penguin.
———. (2012). *The fault in our stars.* New York: Penguin.
Hinton, S. E. (1967). *The outsiders.* New York: Viking Press.
Kantor, M., Valentino, A., & Lennon, S. (2009). *The Amanda project: Invisible i.* New York: HarperCollins.
Kidd, S. M. (2002). *The secret life of bees.* New York: Penguin.
Konigsberg, E. L. (2002). *Silent to the bone.* New York: Aladdin.
Lowry, L. (1993). *The giver.* New York: Houghton Mifflin Harcourt.
McCormick, P. (2006). *Sold.* New York: Hyperion.
Meyers, W. D. (1999). *Monster.* New York: HarperCollins.
———. (2008). *Sunrise over Fallujah.* New York: Scholastic Press.
Nye, N. S. (1997). *Habibi.* New York: Aladdin.
Riordan, R. (2010). *The lightning thief.* New York: Disney Hyperion Books.
———. (2008). *The 39 clues: The maze of bones.* New York: Scholastic.
Ryan, P. M. (2000). *Esperanza rising.* New York: Scholastic.
Soto, G. (1997). *Buried onions.* New York: Harcourt.
Wells, T. (2009). *Mackenzie Blue.* New York: HarperCollins.
Wiesel, E. (1972). *Night.* New York: Farrar, Straus and Giroux.
Zuzsak, M. (2005). *The book thief.* New York: Knopf.

REFERENCES

Alverson, B. (2014). The graphic advantage. *School Library Journal*, September 8. Retrieved from www.slj.com/2014/09/books-media/the-graphic-advantage-teaching-with-graphic-novels

Angay-Crowder, T., Choi, J., & Yi, Y. (2013). Putting multiliteracies into practice: Digital storytelling for multilingual adolescents in a summer program. *TESL Canada Journal*, *30*(2), 37–45.

Bond, E. L. (2011). *Literature and the young adult reader*. Boston: Pearson Education.

Brock, C. H., Goatley, V. J., Raphael, T. E., Trost-Shahata, E., & Weber, C. M. (2014). *Engaging students in disciplinary literacy, K–6*. New York: Teachers College Press.

Bucher, K. T., & Hinton, K. M. (2006). *Young adult literature: Exploration, evaluation, and appreciation*. Boston: Allyn & Bacon.

Bull, K. B. (2011). Connecting with texts: Teacher candidates reading young adult literature. *Theory into Practice, 50*(3), 223–30.

Costello, A., & Reigstad, T. (2014). Approaching young adult literature through multiple literacies. *English Journal, 103*(4), 83–89.

Emig, L. (2015). Combining young adult and classic literature in a secondary English classroom. *Rising Tide, 7*, 4–27.

Gavigan, K. (2012). Caring through comics—graphic novels and bibliotherapy for grades 6–12. *Knowledge Quest, 40*(5), 78–80.

Gibbons, S. L., Dail, J. S., & Stallworth, B. J. (2006, Summer). Young adult literature in the English curriculum today: Classroom teachers speak out. *ALAN Review*, 53–61.

Green, J. (2014). Does young adult mean anything anymore? Genre in a digitized world, *Proceedings from Zena Sutherland Lecture Series*. Chicago: Booklist.

Gunter, G., & Kenny, R. (2008). Digital booktalk: Digital media for reluctant readers. *Contemporary Issues in Technology and Teacher Education, 8*(1), 84–89.

Hill, R. (2010). When technology and books collide: Attracting struggling readers with multi-platform books. *Booklinks*, March, 8–11.

Lawn, Joy. (2012). Frame by frame: Understanding the appeal of the graphic novel for the middle years. *Literacy Learning: The Middle Years, 20*(1), 26–36.

Morocco, C. C., & Hindin, A. (2002). The role of conversation in a thematic understanding of literature. *Learning Disabilities Research & Practice, 17*(3), 144–59.

Palmi, C., Augsburger, D., & Havere, D. (2016). Transforming preservice teachers' awareness and understanding of multiculturalism through the use of young adult literature. *Illinois Reading Council, 44*(4), 12–22.

Robin, B. (2008). Digital storytelling: A powerful technology tool for the 21st century classroom. *Theory into Practice, 47*, 220–28.

Truax, M. (2010/2011). Reaching reluctant readers in middle school. *Illinois Reading Council Journal, 39*(1), 3–10.

Wadham, R. L., & Ostenson, J. W. (2013). *Integrating young adult literature through the Common Core Standards*. Santa Barbara, CA: Libraries Unlimited.

Part II

Strategies, Approaches, and Models for Increasing Literacy Motivation and Achievement

Chapter Five

Aesthetic Approaches for Teaching Writing to Upper Elementary Students

Amanda Gardner and Evan Ditmore

"Learning to write is a matter of learning to shatter the silences, of making meaning, of learning to learn" (Greene, 1995, p. 108). Writing, then, is an organic process that begins in the silences of the student and moves toward expression. However, as Kozol (2005) observes, the current structure of schools and the influence of standardized testing measures leaves little time in urban school sites for the exploration of silenced voices. Instead of learning to learn in these classrooms, students are learning to test. Kozol (2005) asserts that this type of regimented instructional method is highly detrimental in cultivating the academic, social, and cultural values associated with successful education.

Teaching writing on test-driven elementary campuses encourages (sometimes requires) teachers to introduce the essay as a product with a prescribed, formulaic pattern for excellence. This formulaic approach is not always helpful to the teacher. As one urban elementary teacher noted, "I know that many teachers struggle with teaching writing or say they don't know how to teach it. Even being [given] a book and to use it isn't helpful if we are just handed a book and told to teach from a lesson that was written by someone else" (Gardner, personal communication, 2017).

Instead of looking to prescribed writing curricula to help raise test scores, teachers should consider looking at writing from an aesthetic point of view. An aesthetic approach provides teachers with a strategy to help students counter the almost prescribed process demanded by standardized testing, to generate authentic ideas, and to pull early thoughts from the fuzziness of formation to the clarity of composition.

This chapter begins by looking at the current composition practices exemplified by Texas's standardized exam, the State of Texas Assessments of Academic Readiness (STAAR); then considers how prewriting and student voice is constricted by mandated exams; and finally, offers teachers an alternative prewriting strategy in the form of aesthetic education as a counter to the impositions of externally mandated practices.

STANDARDIZED EXAMINATIONS AND CURRENT WRITING EXPECTATIONS

Recent years have added the goal of passing an externally created and graded writing exam to the desired outcomes for students. The pressure created for both staff and students by the need for each child to earn a passing score on the external exam has altered the goal of teaching composition. Whereas the instructional goal used to be helping students to clearly express their own individual thoughts on the subject presented, modern examination practices have added a checklist of "must includes" that will tip a paper from failure to success. This changes the creative art of authentic composition to an assembly-line practice, producing false writing for the expressed purpose of passing an exam.

Because the write-by-numbers approach to language arts, also termed here as "false writing," makes it easier for students to satisfy the demands of standardized testing, and in recognition of the premium placed on student scores for schools, an almost procedural approach to writing pedagogy is benignly coerced (Bennett, 2016; Mabry, 1999). The effects of this perspective toward writing even permeate the way teachers are encouraged to approach its teaching.

The writing problem in upper elementary grades, then, is the very real disconnect between the habits of mind cultivated for successful completion of standardized exams, and those needed for creation of independent compositions. The former, which can be thought of as false writing, requires the ability to reproduce the expected structure and appropriate buzzwords that scorers expect to find; the latter, authentic writing, requires an ability to understand the purpose of composing and to create an appropriate textual response.

False Writing Decoded

Changing how the essay process is approached begins with redefining the purpose of that task. Unlike math, history, and science, students' mastery of composition cannot be tested by multiple choice; instead, students' composition skills must be considered in context of the total essay composed, from diction and syntax to structure and voice. Writing, as indicated by the state test rubrics, relies on those conventions, which can be examined objectively and compared against a set description of what is acceptable and what is not. Mabry (1999), in considering "state mandated direct writing assessment[s]" (p. 673), states:

> Writing rubrics can fail to predict the actual features of a student's writing, thereby creating a mismatch between scoring criteria and actual performance. In cases in which the overall effect of a student's performance is achieved by means not anticipated in the scoring criteria, criterial analysis of the quality of writing will deflect a scorer's attention away from the actual writing, and the score will not support valid inferences about the student's achievement. (p. 677)

Thus, a student essay is scarcely reviewed for its holistic value; instead, only its components are considered, regardless of how well those components fit into the whole.

Ruecker (2013) notes that traditionally marginalized students are disproportionately affected by the pressures associated with standardized testing because their instruction is more likely to consist of a curriculum designed for the sole purpose of test preparation, rather than the development of critical thinking and composition skills.

The STAAR exam's description of the highest score on the fourth-grade writing test illustrates the inauthenticity of the writing process required. STAAR states that a 4 out of 4 is an essay that "represents an accomplished writing performance" (Texas Education Agency, 2016, p. 18). Further, it defines "an accomplished writing performance" through three key areas: "Organization/Progression," "Development of Ideas," and "Use of Language/Conventions" (p. 18). Each of these sections focuses on the end product, and neglects the creation process, a process that is firmly centered in the student.

The STAAR does, however, include specific directions for the students, as shown in figure 5.1.

The half-page STAAR prompt holds three short paragraphs of direction— READ, THINK, WRITE. Each direction emphasizes the linguistic nature of the task. Further, each points to writing as a linear process: first READ the prompt, then THINK about an answer and, finally, WRITE a response that fits in the allotted space. This linear three-step process is the only strategy presented in the exam (Texas Education Agency, 2016).

Moreover, this sequential process presumes that the student will complete this process solely in sequence and solely through language, and discounts the individuality of each student. The further explanation continues this presumption by using "state," "writing," "words," and "spelling, capitalization, punctuation, grammar, and sentences," all verbal processes. This standardized approach to writing can be visualized through the graphic in figure 5.2.

WRITTEN COMPOSITION: Expository

READ the information in the box below.

> When we are young, we often imagine having the chance
> to meet someone we admire.

THINK about having the chance to meet anyone in the world. What person would you choose to meet?

WRITE about the person you would want to meet and explain why you would choose that person.

Be sure to —

- clearly state your central idea
- organize your writing
- develop your writing in detail
- choose your words carefully
- use correct spelling, capitalization, punctuation, grammar, and sentences

Figure 5.1.   Sample STAAR Prompt. This figure was created by the contributing authors.

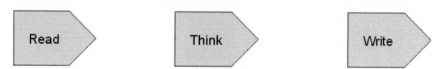

Figure 5.2.   Visual Representation of STAAR Writing Sequence This figure was created by the contributing authors

The graphic illustrates the presumption of only one way to approach composing, and negates the possibility of varied prewriting methods that students of diverse experiences might use in their creation process.

The premium placed on student scores for schools might be one reason this almost procedural approach in essay instruction is stressed in the assessment process. In attempting to guarantee high scores, districts sometimes use professional development to clarify what students need to show in their written responses. This approach to professional development ignores language as an art, full of nuance and subtleties unique to the writer; instead, this type of professional development views composition as a product that can be systematically assembled, like a bookshelf from a box.

The following vignette illustrates one teacher's experience with a score-driven approach to teacher training:

> *Mr. Fitzgerald, an experienced teacher, attended a statewide professional development writing session in 2013. The session was given not by a literacy expert, but by a person who worked to develop his state's test, and who spoke on the topic of how the writing portion of the test is scored.*
>
> *During the course of the day, Mr. Fitzgerald learned that each reader for the essays is allotted roughly sixty seconds to determine the quality of writing. He also learned the key concepts that scorers are looking for to differentiate between a passing and a failing writing sample: transition words such as "first," "next," and "finally"; varied sentence structure; regurgitation of the prompt's language; and correct use of the semicolon.*
>
> *The entire professional development was geared toward teaching him how to help his students avoid a third scorer on a test, not on showing him how to help his students better communicate their ideas in words.*

Though all teachers may not have experienced such a blatantly test-driven professional development session, some educators have recognized how ubiquitous standardized testing has become in their profession, in their curriculum, and in their students' education. However, this does not have to be the reality.

One way to rebel against this reality is to use an aesthetic approach to writing instruction. Such an approach might help teachers satisfy the demands of false writing required by the tests, while eliciting authentic responses from their students.

AESTHETIC FRAME OF MIND FOR TEACHERS

Traditional aesthetic education is understood as Maxine Greene championed it during her time as Philosopher in Residence at the Lincoln Art Center. In 2001, Greene published a collection of her lectures from her tenure there, including an address to teachers she first delivered in 1980 titled "Notes on Aesthetic Education," where she said of aesthetic education: "Most simply, most directly, it is education for more discriminating appreciation and understanding of the several arts" (Greene, 2001, p. 8).

It is through the appreciation and understanding of the arts that students will practice how to see more critically, more closely, and how to pay attention to the ordinary in a state Greene (1977) calls "wide-awakeness" (pp. 120–21), a term she notes she appropriated from philosopher Alfred Schutz.

According to Greene (2001), students need to develop "a more active sensibility and awareness," and that the "starting point" of this is an "ability to feel from the inside what the arts are like and how they mean. Experiences of this sort cannot but become the ground of an illumination of much that lies beyond, and we are preoccupied with allowing such illumination to occur" (p. 8).

This illumination, in the standardized testing education of 2017, is secondary if not tertiary when teacher retention depends on students' scores on external exams (Nichols & Berliner, 2007). Greene (2001) clarifies that "the aesthetic experience is not simply an affair of feeling or sensation or responsiveness to a beat"; it is also "the notion that heightened understanding might well heighten enjoyment and extend the range of what is prized" (p. 9).

Looking at writing through the framework of Greene's aesthetic education allows for teachers to create in their classrooms a truly generative compositional process. As opposed to the product-centered notion presented by contemporary standard makers, the aesthetic concept fully embraces Vygotsky's social constructivist view, whereby learning and the context in which it takes place, are fundamentally inseparable (Vygotsky, 2004). To reiterate, Greene (1995) says, "Learning to write is a matter of learning to shatter the silences, of making meaning, of learning to learn" (p. 108). Thus, a student's essay ability cannot be effectively measured by means of a single, decontextualized performance that addresses a topic intentionally selected for its generic nature and rhetorical simplicity. Doing so would eliminate the element of humanity that both Greene and Vygotsky claimed to be so critical to the process of meaningful learning.

Throughout her works, Greene (2001) reinforces "the connection between cognitive understanding and our capacity to hear and to see and to attend" (p. 9). This ability "to hear and to see and to attend" that which exists in the world is Greene's concept of wide-awakeness. It is this sense of attentiveness to the world that can help upper elementary students create cognitive connections between their experiences, their ideas, and their expression of them in the essay. To do this, however, requires a variation on Greene's aesthetic education. It requires an application of aesthetic education to the writing process.

This variation of aesthetic education opens the possibility for students to look at their own ideas in this heightened sense of wide-awakeness by using the arts to conceptualize, contemplate, and express their thoughts before codifying them verbally. The students become the artists whose attentiveness is directed to their own ideas by using art—drawn, sculpted, performed— prior to linguistic codification.

Using art to access ideas is not a new idea. However, little study has been done at the upper elementary level that focuses on the use of art as a preliminary scaffold for essay construction in a classroom setting. In contrast to the paucity of studies at the upper elementary level, drawing as a prewriting strategy has been studied in connection with narrative and fiction more intensely at the lower elementary level (Dunn, 2013; Dunn & Finley, 2010; Leigh, 2012; Mackenzie, 2011; Mackenzie & Veresov, 2013; Moore & Caldwell, 1993; Steele, 2016).

Dunn and Finley (2010) utilized action research during the At Home At School summer school program for homeless K–8 students in southwest Washington. From the forty-three Thirsty Thinkers Writers' Workshop participants, they reported on three representative cases—one second, one third, and one fourth grader. Each student chose to attend more than once, and was exposed to a narrative story that was assessed with the Ask, Reflect, Text (ART) strategy. In planning their own stories, they applied the same strategy: asking the WWW questions (Who, What, Where), reflecting artistically (drew, painted, sculpted) on their story, and typing their story into a word processing program (Dunn & Finley, 2010, p. 37). The authors reported that all three "demonstrated their interest in writing and a desire to improve their skills" (p. 39).

Leigh (2012) paired with a second-grade teacher to investigate how students' knowledge of specific drawing techniques employed in children's books would impact students' own drawings and, additionally, how the writings created from those drawings would be impacted. Leigh concluded that students exhibited three characteristics from this knowledge: (1) the use of visualization to "extend ideas for writing," (2) a deeper attention to professional techniques and application of those techniques to their own drawings, and (3) experience of "joy in writing" (p. 403). The second finding, "a deeper attention to professional techniques and application of those techniques to their own drawings," is an example of wide-awakeness.

An upper elementary study conducted by Christianakis (2011) considered how one fifth-grade urban class viewed the interplay between text and image, and how classroom and curricular expectations influenced their text creation. Findings "suggest that visual symbols combine with written language to make new meanings, not necessarily linked to the concrete world, but possibly to social, imagined, and critical worlds" (p. 48).

The mingling of image and text to create new meaning is similar to the language within graphic novels (McCloud, 2011); upper elementary students able to think in this multimodal language hold an advantage in modernity's multimedia reality. That the new meanings observed by Christianakis (2011) are linked "possibly to social, imagined, and critical worlds" (p. 48), suggests that students press their own interpretations onto the given in a more active, attentive engagement that indicates a state near wide-awakeness.

The Need for Aesthetic Education

Embracing wide-awakeness, the authentic thought and deliberation so vehemently espoused by Greene, is central to advancing beyond the overly simplistic understanding of writing put forth by various state and national entities through the use of rubrics to codify "good" essays.

Far from the "Production and Distribution of Writing" described by the Common Core State Standards for fourth graders (Common Core State Standards Initiative, 2017), an aesthetic approach to teaching the essay entails introspective exploration on a level that challenges the way one thinks about life itself; to be "made aware of incompleteness and of a human reality to be pursued" (Greene, 1977, p. 123) is necessary for achieving the fullness of expression that writing and the writing process should embody.

Juxtaposed as they may seem, Greene's vision of written expression through aesthetics need not be viewed as the polar opposite of the states' ideas regarding its teaching. Rather, it should be considered that Greene's thoughts might be wholly incorporated into instruction that both satisfies the requirements of the established standards and facilitates the eloquent, articulate, and purposeful communication promulgated by the likes of Dewey (1934/2005) and Greene (1995; 2001).

As is typical of many states' academic standards for language arts, the Common Core State Standards address writing in terms of a process to create a product. Thinking along these lines inevitably leads to adopting a somewhat formulaic approach to written expression; though such methods may be effective for the purpose of satisfying a state's testing requirements, they are hardly conducive to eliciting genuine expression from students. An aesthetic perspective, however, may help alleviate the repression imposed on teachers and students by the rubric-based benchmarks they are so often forced to pursue.

Far removed from Greene's ideas of enlightenment and illumination, the current state of writing instruction exists in a creative vacuum. Because teachers are encouraged to produce test scores rather than writers, essay instruction takes on the procedural existence imposed on it by those who design state writing assessments. Mandatory outlines, paragraphs of uniform length, and stock adjectives are just a few of the hallmarks of compositions in the post–standardized-testing era.

Taking advantage of art's potential to transform students' approaches to crafting a written response to a prompt requires a teacher who is willing to invest time and energy in the creative process. Considering that many students have been exposed only to the scripted style of verbal expression that is required of them by their state's high-stakes testing, it becomes necessary for the teacher to assist in reshaping how students perceive the purpose of producing an essay.

Effectively analyzing and critiquing the work of others is one key to unlocking students' own capacity for articulating their thoughts, ideas, and emotions. Literary elements such as voice, tone, mood, and irony should be explored at a level that goes beyond simple identification; students should recognize creativity and expressiveness as being the hallmarks of quality composition and, in turn, be encouraged to produce it.

Just as all great authors are influenced by the work of their predecessors, students should likewise draw from the artistic efforts of others to learn what makes language powerful. This knowledge, coupled with the use of innovative strategies conducive to the development of an aesthetic frame of mind, promote an understanding of language as a means of conveying and defining one's worldview. In so expressing their worldview, students begin to become attentive to the reality around them and, through this attentiveness, wide awake to their interaction with and agency upon their world.

AESTHETIC POSSIBILITIES IN THE CLASSROOM

Incorporating aesthetic education into prewriting strategies helps replace false writing practices with authentic ones. Though contemporary teachers and students are bound to external standardized exams, they do not have to be tied to the linear, lock-step approach and rote composition practices that exam rubrics induce. Teachers can combat this through employing an aesthetic approach to language arts.

Such an approach starts with teaching students to think differently about writing, to start not with an outline, list, or mind map, but to start with the images and experiences students carry within. Starting the writing process from within prompts authentic writing.

Within this type of aesthetic approach, students who may have been silenced by circumstance become the source material and, as the source material, are recognized for their intrinsic value. Teachers who utilize an aesthetic approach to writing build on that source while teaching their students to pay attention, to notice, to connect. When students are capable of such wide-awakeness, the rote turns remarkable; the standard, sublime; the mundane, magnificent. Aesthetic possibilities in the classroom are limitless.

EXAMPLE AESTHETIC LESSONS

The following examples provide only a small glimpse into the possibilities afforded by the aesthetic approach. In no way should they be seen as wholly representative of the concept itself, nor should they be viewed as the only way to approach these possibilities. Each format will be presented as a general template followed by specific examples.

Possibility I: The Traditional

Traditional aesthetic education seeks to elicit an emotional response to the art from the student through a deep knowledge of the art, the artist, and the era from which it was created.

General Template

> Step 1: The teacher studies an artistic genre and specific works within that genre.
>
> Step 2: The teacher shares that knowledge with students by taking them through one of the works.
>
> Step 3: The teacher chooses another work and prompts students to use prior knowledge to assess the work.
>
> Step 4: The teacher asks students to create an original work in the style of the artist.
>
> Step 5: Students explain their art to their teacher or to each other.
>
> Step 6: Students write an original composition describing their art or a comparison with the original. Students could also write a reflection on their process of using their own images to prompt their words.

Specific Example

> Step 1: Study the Impressionists. Focus on Vincent van Gogh and *Starry Night*, *Self-Portrait*, and *Bedroom in Arles*.
>
> Step 2: Create a lesson on Impressionism that focuses on Van Gogh's life and style. Use *Starry Night* to exemplify his style. Include images of the whole painting and sequential close-ups.
>
> Step 3: Provide images of the whole painting and sequential close-ups for both *Self-Portrait* and *Bedroom in Arles*. Guide a class discussion on one of them. With the other, ask students in small groups or pairs to examine the work and then pull them into a whole group discussion.
>
> Step 4: Provide the class with art supplies and ask students to create their own work—a landscape, a portrait, or a still life—mimicking Van Gogh's style.
>
> Step 5: Have students present their work, asking them to explain how the work they created matched what they hoped to create.
>
> Step 6: Have students use their painting as a reference to write a description of what they created, reminding them to go back to their art for accuracy, or have students compare their work to the original and explain the differences.

Possibility II: The Imagistic

Here, the aesthetic approach to writing begins with the student. Instead of looking at an external work of art and responding, the student creates original art in response to a given prompt. In other words, their prewriting is predrawing (or presketching, prepainting, presculpting, precollaging, or prediorama-ing). Regardless of what form the precreation takes, it originates with the student and with the images unique to that student's life experience.

General Template

Step 1: Give a specific writing prompt that allows for different opinions to be voiced.

Step 2: Direct students to brainstorm their responses to the prompt with images. Three-dimensional products such as sculpture or origami could also be used if the resources are available.

Step 3: Ask students to choose one idea and depict it artistically.

Step 4: Instruct students to use their art as a reference for their written response.

Step 5: Have students "edit" their written response by returning to their art for comparison with their artistic creation.

Example Prompts

Geography

a. Consider the location of where we live. Consult the given map/s and note the geographical features of this area. Then, in an essay, explain how these features contributed to the settlement of our area. Alternatively, create a brochure or a guide for these features describing their importance to our town.

History

a. In your opinion, what is the most important Amendment to the Constitution? Explain why it is the most important.

b. Create a written explanation of the positive outcomes resulting from the free enterprise system.

Language Arts

a. Consider Natalie Babbitt's *Tuck Everlasting* (1975). Explain Babbitt's theme. Be certain to reference the text.

b. In a graphic, using *both* image and sentences, illustrate the reasons why being in fifth grade is great.

c. In an essay, describe your favorite childhood memory.

Math

a. In a letter, explain the importance of learning geometry to someone who doesn't want to study the subject.

b. Thoroughly describe the Pythagorean Theorem and how it can be proven.

Science

    a. Thoroughly describe one type of energy (light, mechanical, thermal, electrical, or sound). Include in your description its properties and uses.

    b. In an essay, compare how plants and animals create energy.

Possibility III: The Dramatic

As with the imagistic variation, the dramatic approach to writing also begins with the students. Although an imagistic approach can be made collaborative, the dramatic approach is intrinsically collaborative, kinesthetic, and nonverbal. This prewriting strategy has students share their interpretation of the idea with their classmates, and compare the interpretations before going to the written. Acting out the idea requires clarity of concept that should translate to the written text.

    Although this approach might be daunting to use, its potential benefits are worth the initial trepidation. Asking students to act out an idea allows them to collaborate with classmates, which assists in clarification and learning; it provides a safe activity for the more dramatic students while stretching shy students from their comfort zone. An example of this lesson is found in the following vignette of a seasoned fourth-grade teacher.

> *For the summative assessment over photosynthesis, Mrs. Shelly would place her students in groups of five, a number she chose so that each student in the group would have a role in the drama: sun, chlorophyll, water, carbon dioxide, nutrients (earth or soil). She did not tell them what roles there were, only that they would have to act out the process of photosynthesis, that every group member had to act, and that they were not allowed to speak—their actions would have to show her that they understood photosynthesis.*
>
>   *After ample time to discuss and then practice, every group performed before the class. During the performances, students in the audience were asked to look for the different stages of photosynthesis; then, between performances, differences and similarities were discussed. At the end of everyone's play, Mrs. Shelly facilitated a whole class discussion.*

To extend Mrs. Shelly's activity to composition, students could then be directed to describe photosynthesis, perhaps with an accompanying illustration of the steps involved. They could also be asked to compare how their part was acted by members of other groups to their own interpretation, noting how accurately each interpretation remained to the original's purpose. For example, how did each student become the Sun? How did the reviewer? What could the reviewer have added? At what did the reviewer excel?

General Dramatic Template

Step 1: Place students in groups appropriate for the task.

Step 2: Give students a prompt or direction for focus.

Step 3: Instruct students to show the concept dramatically. Depending on the students, this might mean without words.

Step 4: Have groups perform the concept for the class.

Step 5: Lead a discussion assessing the different interpretations.

Step 6: Ask students to answer the prompt or explain the concept in an essay.

FINAL THOUGHTS: A WAY FORWARD

Incorporating an aesthetic frame of mind into prewriting strategies of upper elementary students provides a nonverbal platform on which students can build their writing fluency. Because an aesthetic approach to writing asks that students pull from their own experiences, traditionally silenced populations are encouraged to become vocal.

Asking students to be wide awake, to pay attention to the ideas they generate in images while they translate them to text, helps to foster a habit of attentiveness in gaining agency as they mature.

Beyond the attentiveness to their own work, creating images from their own experiences serves as a point of validation. Further, it requires that students reflect on ways in which they feel silenced, and how they derive meaning from their experience(s). In deciding to use an aesthetic approach to writing with their students, teachers choose to replace false writing practices with authentic writing processes and are empowering students to "shatter the silences" of their situation(s) to add narrative and voice to the larger composition of America.

REFERENCES

Babbit, N. (1975). *Tuck everlasting.* New York: Farrar, Straus & Giroux.

Bennett, C. (2016). Assessment rubrics: Thinking inside the boxes. *Learning and Teaching*, *9*(1), 50–72.

Christianakis, M. (2011). Children's text development: Drawing, pictures, and writing. *Research in the Teaching of English*, *46*(1), 22–54.

Common Core State Standards Initiative. (2017). Preparing America's students for success. Retrieved fromhttp://www.corestandards.org/

Dewey, J. (1934/2005). *Art as experience.* New York: Perigee.

Dunn, M. (2013). Using art media during prewriting: Helping students with dysgraphia manage idea generation before encoding text. *Exceptionality*, *21*(4), 224–37.https://doi.org/10.1080/09362835.2013.802234

Dunn, M. W., & Finley, S. (2010). Children's struggles with the writing process: Exploring storytelling, visual arts, and keyboarding to promote narrative story writing. *Multicultural Education, 18*(1), 33–42.

Greene, M. (1977). Toward wide-awakeness: An argument for the arts and humanities in education. *Teachers College Record: New York, NY, 79*(1), 119. Retrieved from http://search.proquest.com/docview/1311540328?pq-origsite=summon

———. (1995). *Releasing the imagination: Essays on education, the arts, and social change.* San Francisco: Jossey-Bass.

———. (2001). *Variations on a blue guitar: The Lincoln Center Institute lectures on aesthetic education.* New York: Teachers College Press.

Kozol, J. (2005). *The shame of the nation: The restoration of apartheid schooling in America.* New York: Three Rivers Press.

Leigh, S. R. (2012). Writers draw visual hooks: Children's inquiry into writing. *Language Arts, 89*(6), 396–404. Retrieved fromhttp://www.jstor.org/stable/41804362

Mabry, L. (1999). Writing to the rubric: Lingering effects of traditional standardized testing on direct writing assessment. *Phi Delta Kappan, 80*(9), 673–79. Retrieved from https://eric.ed.gov/?id=EJ585679

Mackenzie, N. (2011). From drawing to writing: What happens when you shift teaching priorities in the first six months of school? *Australian Journal of Language and Literacy, 34*(3), 322. Retrieved fromhttp://go.galegroup.com.ezproxy.baylor.edu/ps/i.do?p=GRGM&u=txshracd2488&id=GALE%7CA269531624&v=2.1&it=r&sid=summon&userGroup=txshracd2488&authCount=1#

Mackenzie, N., & Veresov, N. (2013). How drawing can support writing acquisition: Text construction in early writing from a Vygotskian perspective. *Australasian Journal of Early Childhood, 33*(4), 22. Retrieved fromhttp://go.galegroup.com/ps/i.do?p=GRGM&sw=w&u=txshracd2488&v=2.1&it=r&id=GALE%7CA357035147&sid=summon&asid=c3d826d45d1cd783ac90d8281c6d0ef7

McCloud, S. (2011). *Understanding comics: The invisible art.* New York: HarperPerennial.

Moore, B. H., & Caldwell, H. (1993). Drama and drawing for narrative writing in primary grades. *Journal of Educational Research, 87*(2), 100–110. Retrieved fromhttp://search.proquest.com.ezproxy.baylor.edu/docview/1290440737/citation/184F43971E64FE2PQ/1

Nichols, S. L., & Berliner, D. C. (2007). *Collateral damage: How high-stakes testing corrupts America's schools.* Cambridge, MA: Harvard Education Press.

Ruecker, T. (2013). High-stakes testing and Latina/o students: Creating a hierarchy of college readiness. *Journal of Hispanic Higher Education, 12*(4), 303–20.

Steele, J. S. (2016). Becoming creative practitioners: Elementary teachers tackle artful approaches to writing instruction. *Teaching Education, 27*(1), 72–87. https://doi.org/10.1080/10476210.2015.1037829

Texas Education Agency. (2016). *Grade 4 writing: Expository writing guide March 2016.* Retrieved fromwww.tea.texas.gov/WorkArea/DownloadAsset.aspx?id=51539610795

Vygotsky, L. S. (2004). Imagination and creativity in childhood. *Journal of Russian & East European Psychology, 42*(1), 7–97. Retrieved fromhttp://ezproxy.baylor.edu/login?url=http://search.ebscohost.com/login.aspx?direct=true&db=pbh&AN=12312275&site=ehost-live&scope=site

Chapter Six

The 3CO Approach to
Writing Instruction

Nancy P. Gallavan and Gloria Loring

Writing instruction with third-grade elementary school students, particularly students in schools in urban settings, requires classroom teachers to be equipped with an abundant repertoire of rich, powerful, diverse, culturally relevant, and developmentally appropriate content and pedagogy. Likewise, teachers must be empowered with a comprehensive knowledge of their students, their students' settings, and their students' successes and struggles culturally, academically, cognitively, socially, physically, and affectively, both in and out of the classroom and school.

Ultimately, teachers must be curious, receptive, enlightened, and compassionate as they embark on enhancing their own self-efficacy to increase student engagement and achievement associated with the teaching, learning, and schooling. Tending to teach the way they were taught, primarily in suburban and rural settings, teachers in urban settings too often teach according to their own long-held beliefs and strongly ingrained expectations about their students and settings (Gallavan, 2007).

Additionally, most classroom teachers are not prepared to teach writing as they attempt to fulfill school district mandates. However, the guidance and support of an effective mentor (Wang & Odell, 2003) for co-exploring new possibilities and co-constructing new knowledge are essential.

Collaboratively, a university professor and a third-grade classroom teacher working in an urban setting developed the 3CO Approach to Writing Instruction. This chapter details the 3CO Approach they co-constructed and implemented in the teacher's elementary classroom, and their findings related to improved writing instruction and teacher self-efficacy.

The 3CO Approach is student-centered, inquiry-based, and authentically illuminating, capitalizing upon culturally responsive pedagogy (Gay, 2002; Ladson-Billings, 1992) and students' cultural funds of knowledge (Gonzáles, Moll, & Amanti, 2005) to enhance the teacher's sense of self-efficacy (Bandura, 1977; Tschannen-Moran, & Woolfolk Hoy, 2007).

Authentic and holistic experiences can increase student motivation, engagement, productivity, and achievement in compliance with requirements established by school administrators and classroom teachers. Specifically, and ideally, state frameworks and curricular models should ensure that writing instruction in elementary school classrooms is featured as an independent content area coupled with concepts and practices of writing instruction integrated across the curriculum.

URBAN SETTINGS AND TEACHING

Darling-Hammond (as cited in Milner & Lomotey, 2013, p. xi) describes an urban setting as a "densely populated area, generally created as a hub of commerce and transport, and often—as a consequence—a location where people have come from many other places, representing diverse geographic and, increasingly, linguistic, ethnic, and racial origins. The intermingling of peoples, customs, and ideas often brings a cosmopolitan edge . . . that distinguishes their institutions and their people." Darling-Hammond continues, "However, in contemporary U.S. society, urban has come to connote places where the changing economy has left many families behind, where poverty and segregation are concentrated, and where severely under-resourced schools struggle to meet the increasingly intense needs of their students and families" (cited in Milner & Lomotey, 2013, p. xi.).

Too often, the term "urban setting" tends to convey negative images of difficult, if not undesirable, social conditions such as an abundance of lower-income and/or impoverished residents living in higher density homes, and increased levels of racial, ethnic, and religious diversity. The term also connotes decreased numbers of two-parent and nuclear families; increased numbers of parents working night hours; lower levels of parental care about schools, education, community, and country; and higher levels of noise, trash, violence, and blight (Haberman, 2004). "Such negative associations with the term urban profoundly affect education and shape the nature of urban schooling" (Haberman, 2004 as cited in Armstrong & McMahon, 2006, p. x). Without factual data, realistic portrayals, and actual experiences in urban settings with local residents, these images frequently overwhelm people who do not live in urban settings, such as teacher candidates, policy makers, and media journalists, and their strongly held beliefs about teaching, learning, and schooling in urban settings (Gilbert, 1997).

Teaching in Urban Settings

Most elementary teachers working in urban schools were not raised in urban settings (Wang & Odell, 2003). As P–12 students raised in suburban or rural settings, elementary school teachers who work in schools in urban settings tend to bring their preexisting experiences and perceptions related to teaching, learning, and schooling, especially their beliefs related to their students who frequently are unlike the teachers racially, culturally, and geographically.

In addition, elementary school teachers' preexisting experiences and perceptions may be inconsistent with current academic expectations, literacy content, and culturally relevant pedagogy (Wang & Odell, 2003). Some elementary school teachers may be reluctant, if not resistant, to considering or incorporating new ideas and practices associated with their approaches and attitudes toward teaching students in schools in urban settings (Wang & Odell, 2003).

Thus, the roles of initial teacher preparation and continuous professional development are significant for establishing and promoting teachers' reflections, receptiveness, and responsiveness for enhancing their self-efficacy. Wang and Odell (2003) found that reform-minded mentors, in particular, helped teacher candidates and novice teachers transform their ideas and practices about literacy content and pedagogical strategies associated with writing instruction in schools in urban settings. Mentors must be ready to intercede with teacher candidates and colleagues to redirect writing instruction to optimize student learning and to strengthen teacher practices that benefit the schooling holistically.

WRITING INSTRUCTION

Writing instruction encompasses knowledge, skills, and dispositions necessary for communicating, that is, recording information and expressing thoughts to oneself, to and with others, and about society, in various contexts, including academic, domestic, social, and creative situations. According to the National Council of Teachers of English (NCTE), "writing grows out of many purposes . . . is embedded in complex social relationships and their appropriate languages . . . and . . . occurs in different modalities and technologies" (NCTE, 2016, pp. 1–3). "Writing includes . . . conventions of finished and edited texts as important dimensions of the relationships between writers and readers . . . and emphasizes that . . . everyone has the capacity to write; writing can be taught; and teachers can help students become better writers" (NCTE, 2016, pp. 4–6). As students are learning to write, they also are writing to learn (Gallavan, Bowles, & Young, 2003); their writing tends to parallel their cultural development (Sokol, 2009) and intellectual growth (Mullin, 1998) as they progress from emergent to early to transitional to fluent writers (NCTE, 2016). Elementary school students in various milieu, particularly urban settings, are both augmented by and limited in their cultural development and intellectual growth due to the quality and quantity of guidance and support received both at home and at school (Ntelioglou, Fannin, Montanera, & Cummins, 2014; Sandstrom & Huerta, 2013).

As educators in school districts across the United States strive to increase literacy levels of all students, many reforms in writing instruction have been reported (Graham, McKeown, Kiuhara, & Harris, 2012; Strickland et al., 2001). Typically, in elementary school and middle school classrooms, the formulaic process approach—that is, draft, edit, revise, and redraft—is accompanied by only partial and inconsistent emphasis on the quality and quantity of the teacher's feedback (Matsumura, Patthey-Chavez, Valdés, & Garnier, 2002). High quality and frequently exchanged feedback is desirable and is reflective of culturally responsive pedagogy (Gay, 2002; Ladson-Billings, 1992; Milner, 2011 that acknowledges and builds on each student's academic readiness and cultural fund of knowledge (Gonzáles, Moll, & Amanti, 2005). Milner (2011) ascertains that culturally responsive pedagogy is a broad construct that individual teachers must realize in the context of their own backgrounds, experiences, and beliefs, balanced with the responsibilities for preparing their students as individuals and as members of various groups and of society at large for their futures—that is, college, career, and citizenship.

Effective teachers are dedicated to actualizing critical consciousness (Milner, 2011) evident in teaching, learning, and schooling. Specifically, Delpit (1988) reasons that language is a construct of power in schools; in other words, the teachers and students who recognize that the rules are participatory and become enactors of the rules tend to govern the structure. Teachers must be cognizant of their power over students, as well as recognizing students who govern and the students who are governed, to ensure that everyone—teachers and students—are active participants who understand the rules and are comfortable making informed choices independently.

Concomitantly, Winn and Johnson (2011) advocate that teachers must become fully acquainted with their students' academic readiness and cultural funds of knowledge (Gonzáles, Moll, & Amanti, 2005); as teachers develop their writing instruction, they must consciously consider the world from their students' perspectives and experiences. Collaboratively, teachers and students must engage in advancing curiosity and creativity while co-exploring new possibilities and co-constructing new knowledge.

When the learning becomes student-centered, inquiry-driven, and authentically illuminating, combining the journey and the destination, students (*and teachers*) begin to take more responsibility, ownership, and excitement related to both success and struggle.

The authors of this chapter assert that when the teacher grounds writing instruction in the presence and power of intellectual growth and academic development, together with culturally responsive pedagogy and students' cultural funds of knowledge, then student motivation, engagement, production, and achievement increase and, respectively, fuel future successes that help students *and teachers* overcome struggles.

THE 3CO WRITING PROJECT

Most U.S. third-grade classrooms feature writing instruction; however, writing scores continue to reflect the challenges many elementary school teachers encounter when trying to increase literacy levels of their students, especially students in schools in urban settings. For this research, a third-grade teacher in a school in an urban setting and a university teacher educator serving as a mentor (hereafter called researchers), examined the teacher's writing instruction with the goals of (1) improving writing instruction, (2) increasing writing outcomes emphasizing importance and comprehension, and (3) enhancing teacher self-efficacy.

The researchers investigated the following question: *How can a school district's approach to writing instruction be modified to increase student engagement and achievement to enhance teacher self-efficacy?* Then, capitalizing on the teacher-mentor model (Rowley, 1999), the researchers acknowledged six qualities of an effective mentor to strengthen their relationship: (1) commitment, (2) acceptance, (3) instructional support, (4) differentiated interpersonal contexts, (5) continuous learning, and (6) hope and optimism.

The researchers met four times throughout the school year. During the first meeting, the teacher described current classroom writing instruction, the setting, the students, successes, and struggles. The researchers identified the six factors impacting writing instruction in the classroom, and the four components of student learning that the teacher and mentor would discuss during their research. The researchers then designed the five steps of data collection.

During the second meeting, the researchers collaboratively co-constructed the 3CO Approach to Writing Instruction. During the third meeting, the teacher implemented the 3CO Approach to Writing Instruction in the classroom. During the fourth meeting, the teacher reflected on the design of the research, co-construction of the model, and implementation of the approach in the context of the three goals: (1) improving writing instruction, (2) increasing writing outcomes emphasizing importance and comprehension, and (3) enhancing teacher self-efficacy.

Data was collected via student pre-assessments, student post-assessments, and teacher reflective conversations. Collecting data before and after each unit of writing generated data that the researchers could analyze for validity and reliability. At each of the four meetings, the researchers asked many questions of one another and the conversations flowed comfortably, reflecting the six qualities of an effective mentor.

Context of the Study

All writing instruction occurred in a third-grade classroom located in an elementary school in an urban setting in a school district located in a large capital city in the mid-south region of the United States. This third-grade classroom was one of three third-grade classrooms in an elementary school of five hundred students serving pre-kindergarten through fifth grade.

Writing scores across this school district were below the national average (National Center for Educational Statistics, 2015), and students' writing scores at this school fell into the lowest percentile for the state (Elementary and Secondary Education Act, 2015).

The high school reported a graduation rate of approximately 79 percent, slightly lower than the state average of 85 percent and the national average of 83 percent (Governing the States & Localities, n.d.). The school district tended to experience higher than average turnover, with many new teachers staying only a few years. Although teachers were provided professional development generally related to curricular content, little attention was focused specifically on students and conditions experienced in urban settings, or providing supportive mentoring for the teachers.

The third-grade classroom contained nineteen students: six female and thirteen male. The students' age range was average for third grade, although one student who transferred with no school records may have repeated a grade. The racial distribution of the students included seven African American students, five Hispanic students (all of whom were English Language Learners), two Native American students, and five white students. Reflective of the school and school district population, approximately 95 percent of the students participated in the free and reduced lunch program.

The academic ability range for this third-grade class included two special education students, five gifted/talented students, and a composite reading level of basic or below basic at the beginning of the school year. The teacher reported that participation by parents/families in her school conferences was 100 percent, a much higher rate than reported by all other teachers at this school. Unique to this teacher was dedication to conferencing with families; the teacher offered three ways for parents/families to conference: (1) in person at school, (2) on the phone, or (3) in person at the student's/family's home.

This third-grade teacher had eight years of experience teaching first, third, or fourth grade. She began her career and taught all seven previous years at one other elementary school in the same school district. Teaching was a second career for her; she spent twenty years in the military prior to earning her master of arts in teaching (MAT) degree.

As part of a university MAT program, the teacher taught for two years with a provisional license as an MAT teacher candidate. This teacher became acquainted with her mentor during her time in the MAT program.

First Project Meeting

At the first project meeting, the researchers developed six guidelines to improve writing instruction and increase writing outcomes. The teacher and students would (1) allocate daily time for writing, (2) use an established writing approach, and (3) continuously advance the understanding and application of writing mechanics.

Additionally, guidelines included the need to (4) write for a variety of purposes, with time and structures for self-assessment with proofreading and reflection; (5) share the writing process and writing products with peers; and (6) provide conferencing and feedback with the teacher and student.

Second, the researchers established six reasons why writing was important: writing offered (1) "a valuable mechanism for maintaining personal links with family, friends, and colleagues when we are unable to be with them in person"; (2) "a powerful tool for influencing others"; and (3) "an indispensable medium for learning and communicating" (Graham & Harris, 2013, pp. 5–6).

Moreover, writing provided (4) a reliable means for remembering and understanding material that we have read and heard, especially with narrative and expository text; (5) a significant influence on improving reading, writing, spelling, and communication abilities; and (6) a fulfilling practice to express our daily observations, critical thinking, creative imaginations, and personal thoughts and beliefs.

Third, the researchers clarified a definition of comprehension. For this study, comprehension combined concrete objects and abstract concepts identified and described by specific shared language, and situated in a specific shared context.

Fourth, the researchers formed a description related to enhancing teacher self-efficacy. Based on the research of Bandura (1977), for this study, teacher self-efficacy encompassed the teacher's capacity to be confident in her teaching, the learning of her students, and the changes made to the approaches to the writing instruction to benefit the schooling holistically.

Last, the researchers designed the five steps in data collection, as shown in table 6.1.

Second Project Meeting

During step 2, the researchers co-constructed the 3CO Approach to Writing Instruction with the model shown in figure 6.1.

Third Project Meeting

During step 3, the 3CO Approach to Writing Instruction was implemented. As shown in figure 6.1, this approach was comprised of three stages—Connections, Curiosity, and Creativity (3C). All three stages related to an Object (O) placed at the center of the approach.

Object-based writing instruction was selected for this study due to the teacher's seven years of experiences (the structures, successes, and struggles) with her elementary students in a school in an urban setting. The basic skills of writing were not evident in the students' samples, so the teacher was seeking an approach with structures, functions, directions, and self-expression she could associate with motivation, engagement, productivity, and achievement.

Cognizant of culturally responsive pedagogy (Gay, 2002; Ladson-Billings, 1992) and cultural funds of knowledge (Gonzáles, Moll, & Amanti, 2005), the teacher needed an approach to writing instruction that would maximize her students' potential and mentoring.

Co-construction of the object-based writing instruction allowed the researchers to focus on the basics of description, explanation, and justification of concrete objects, which the teacher could use to guide the students in writing about concrete experiences, such as instructions and processes. The teacher was aware that her students needed to be able to incorporate abstract concepts and principles into their writing too; however, the teacher needed to introduce and reinforce concrete, operational descriptions, explanations, and justifications first.

Mentoring provided the rejuvenation that the teacher needed. Through the researchers' conversations and her fortified classroom practices, the teacher reinforced her strengths and conquered her struggles by being curious, recep-

Table 6.1.   Five Steps of Data Collection

Step 1	Object-based Writing Instruction Implementation aligned with School District; Approach before Mentoring
Step 2	Pre-assessment
Step 3	Object-based Writing Instruction Implementation modified after Pre-assessment and Mentoring
Step 4	Post-assessment
Step 5	Reflection during Mentoring

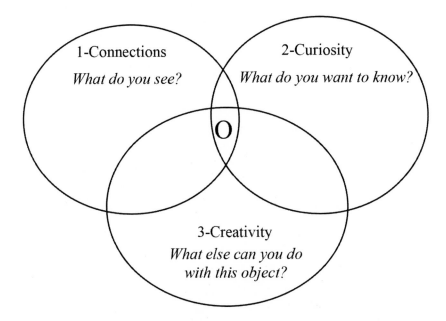

Figure 6.1. 3CO Approach to Writing Instruction Model. This figure was created by the contributing authors.

tive, enlightened, and compassionate about the teaching, learning, and schooling.

Box 6.1 shows an example of the 3CO Approach to Writing Instruction ten-day sequence in relationship to the third-grade teacher's school district writing instruction five-day sequence.

BOX 6.1. 3CO APPROACH TO WRITING INSTRUCTION
EXAMPLE

Day 1: Connections: *What do you see?*

Asking this question, the teacher showed the third graders a wooden object approximately 5 inches long, 1.5 inches wide, and 1/8 inch thick. The wooden object was decorated with a repeating pattern of chevrons approximately 1/2 inch wide carved into the length of the object. The ends of the object were curved, and one end had a hole carved into it with a short piece of leather tied through the hole and knotted with a tan bead.

On their sticky notes students recorded ideas, emphasizing their individual connections including feather, ruler, decoration, musical instrument, nail file, bookmark, cat toy, and tool; these were shared with peers in small groups. However, the teacher did not confirm or deny any of the ideas.

Day 2: Curiosities: *What do you want to know?*

In response to this question, students recorded with their own questions, emphasizing their curiosity including: Does the object have a special job? Does the object have a special meaning? Does the object come in different colors? Does the object come in different sizes? Is the object used by boys or girls, or both? Is the object used by children or adults, or both? How much does the object cost? Do most people have this object? Does the bead have a purpose?

Day 3: Reveal and Introduce the Object; Creativity: *What else can the object do?*

The teacher told the students that this object is a wooden bookmark carved to look like a feather, and that she bought the bookmark in a gift shop in New Mexico that sold Native American items. After answering questions recorded by students the previous day and asked by students on this day, students were provided notepaper to begin writing words and phrases associated with their own ideas for designing, making, and using bookmarks, emphasizing creativity. Students also were provided paper to draw pictures of their objectives.

Day 4: Start Draft on Own

Students continued writing their drafts.

Day 5: Continue Draft on Own, with Peer and/or Group

Students shared their drafts with a peer or group to enhance their paragraphs.

Day 6: Proofread and Revise on Own

Students reread their essays, and made appropriate revisions based on feedback from peers the previous day.

Day 7: Exchange and Revise with Peer

Students traded essays with one another and made revisions together.

Day 8: Edit with Teacher based on Feedback

Students shared their essays with the teacher, and made appropriate revisions based on their one-on-one feedback.

Day 9: Present

Students read their essays aloud to the whole class and shared their pictures. The class was reminded to display effective listening skills.

Day 10: Publish

Students typed their essays with the assistance of the teacher and para-professional. All of the essays with their pictures were combined into a class book. Each student took the class book home to share with their families.

Fourth Project Meeting

Essential to the effectiveness of the 3CO Approach to Writing Instruction were three sets of data gleaned from the pre-assessment, post-assessment, and reflection conversations. The researchers identified gaps and overlaps in the teacher's writing instruction associated with establishing compelling purposes and instilling exciting motivations for improving writing instruction, increasing writing outcomes, and enhancing teacher self-efficacy.

Specifically, with the 3CO Approach to Writing Instruction, the teacher communicated academic expectations more clearly with her students and their families. She planned realistic expectations for the time allocations, wrote specific daily directions that were achievable by the teacher and most students, and continued student activities from one day to the next, ensuring student readiness and understanding. Ultimately, the teacher enhanced her writing instruction via differentiation by aligning her culturally responsive pedagogical practices with each student's cultural funds of knowledge.

Post-assessment data confirmed that students were more motivated, engaged, and productive, contributing to achievement. Achievement was evident during writing instruction as well as across the curriculum. The teacher also reflected that students applied the 3CO Approach to Writing Instruction during the spring standardized testing period, with noticeable improvement in their scores.

FINAL THOUGHTS: BENEFITS OF THE 3CO APPROACH TO WRITING INSTRUCTION

Created so that writing could become both pleasurable and productive, the 3CO Approach to Writing Instruction allows teachers to transform their classrooms into spaces where students can explore newness associated with the unlimited items, ideas, and individuality (Skerrett & Bomer, 2011).

Students discover the power of making choices and expressing their voices (Ray & Laminack, 2001) in ways that are both safe and accepted, as well as dynamic and realistic. If teachers are genuinely supportive of their students (Knoblauch & Woolfolk Hoy, 2008) and their students' writing, the students are far more likely to experience success, not only in writing but across the curriculum (Meyer & Turner, 2002).

All P–12 teachers are preparing their students for life and for opportunities to participate fully in college, career, and citizenship. Essential in all three capacities is the ability to be literate, specifically to communicate through writing, to achieve economic security, and to enjoy holistic well-being.

Therefore, writing is a civil right (Lipman, 2008, p. 62); all teachers, especially elementary school teachers in urban classrooms, must ensure that their students receive equitable information, access, and opportunity to fulfill the academic expectations by co-exploring new horizons and co-constructing new knowledge with their students and, ultimately, challenging and changing both their students and themselves.

The 3CO Approach to Writing Instruction described in this chapter proved to increase teacher self-efficacy (Tschannen-Moran & Woolfolk Hoy, 2007; Viel-Ruma, Houchins, Jolivette, & Benson, 2010; Woolfolk Hoy & Burke Spero, 2005), particularly with attention to student motivation, engagement, productivity, and achievement.

Likewise, the process of co-exploring new possibilities and co-constructing the model proved to enhance the third-grade classroom teacher's sense of self-efficacy. Reflecting on the writing process with her mentor (Murrell, 2001) enabled the teacher to rethink her roles and responsibilities as cultural broker and agent of change (Abbate-Vaughn, 2006), using culturally relevant and developmentally appropriate content and pedagogy with her third-grade students.

REFERENCES

Abbate-Vaughn, J. (2006). "Not writing it out, but writing it off": Preparing multicultural teachers for urban classrooms. *Multicultural Education, 13*(4), 41–48.

Armstrong, D. E., & McMahon, B. J. (2006). *Inclusion in urban educational environments: Addressing issues of diversity, equity, and social justice.* Greenwich, CT: Information Age Publishing.

Bandura, A. (1977). Self-efficacy: Toward a unifying theory of behavior change. *Psychological Review, 84*(2), 191–215.

Delpit, L. D. (1988). The silenced dialogue: Power and pedagogy of teaching other people's children. *Harvard Educational Review, 58*(3), 280–89.

Elementary and Secondary Education Act. (2015). 2015 ESEA School Report. Retrieved from https://s3.amazonaws.com/filespublic/4/docs/educational-accountability/2014-2015-esea/oakbrooke.pdf

Gallavan, N. P. (2007). Seven perceptions that influence novice teachers' efficacy and cultural competence. *Journal of Praxis in Multicultural Education, 2*(1), 6–22.

Gallavan, N. P., Bowles, F. A., & Young, C. T. (2003). Learning to writing; writing to learn: Insights from teacher candidates. *Action in Teacher Education, 29*(2), 61–69.

Gay, G. (2002). Preparing for culturally responsive teaching. *Journal of Teacher Education 53*(2), 106–16.

Gilbert, S. L. (1997). The "four commonplaces of teaching": Prospective teachers' beliefs about teaching in urban schools. *Urban Review, 29*(2), 81–96.

Gonzáles, N., Moll, L. C., & Amanti, C. (2005). Introduction: Theorizing practices. In N. Gonzales, L. C. Moll, and C. Amanti (Eds.), *Funds of knowledge; theorizing practices in households, communities, and classrooms* (pp. 1–28). Mahwah, NJ: Lawrence Erlbaum.

Governing the States & Localities. (n.d.). High school graduation rates by dates. Retrieved from http://www.governing.com/gov-data/high-school-graduation-rates-by-state.html

Graham, S., & Harris, K. R. (2013). Best Practices in Teaching Planning. In S. Graham, C. A. MacArthur, & J. Fitzgerald (Eds.), *Best practices in writing instruction* (2nd ed) (pp. 119–40). New York: Guilford Press.

Graham, S., McKeown, D., Kiuhara, S., & Harris, K. R. (2012). A meta-analysis of writing instruction for students in the elementary grades. *Journal of Educational Psychology, 104*(4), 879–96.

Haberman, M. (2004). Urban education: The state of urban schooling at the start of the 21st century. Retrieved from http://www.habermanfoundation.org/Articles/Default.aspx?id=1

Knoblauch, D., & Woolfolk Hoy, A. (2008). "Maybe I can teach *those* kids": The influence of contextual factors on student teachers' efficacy beliefs. *Teaching and Teacher Education, 24*(1), 166–79.

Ladson-Billings, G. (1992). Liberatory consequences of literacy: A case for culturally relevant instruction for African American students. *Journal of Negro Education, 61*(3), 378–91.

Lipman, P. (2008). Education policy, race, and neoliberalism. In S. Greene (Ed.), *Literacy as a civil right: Reclaiming social justice in literacy teaching and learning* (pp. 45–64). New York: Peter Lang.

Matsumura, L. C., Patthey-Chavez, G. G., Valdés, R., & Garnier, H. (2002). Teacher feedback, writing assignment quality, and third-grade students' revision in lower- and higher-achieving urban schools. *Elementary School Journal, 103*(1), 3–25.

Meyer, D. K., & Turner, J. C. (2002). Discovering emotion in classroom motivation research. *Educational Psychologist, 37*(2), 107–14.

Milner, H. R., IV, & Lomotey, K. (2013). *Handbook of urban education.* New York: Routledge Taylor & Francis.

Milner, H. R., IV. (2011). Culturally relevant pedagogy in a diverse urban classroom. *Urban Review, 43*(1), 66–89.

Mullin, A. E. (1998). Another look at student writing and stages of intellectual development. *Journal of College Reading and Learning, 28*(2), 79–92.

Murrell, P. (2001). *The community teacher: A new framework for effective urban teaching.* New York: Teachers College Press.

National Center for Educational Statistics (NCES). (2015). Highlights of performance of fourth-grade students on the 2012 NAEP Computer-Based Pilot Writing Assessment. Retrieved from https://nces.ed.gov/nationsreportcard/pubs/writing/2015119.aspx

National Council of Teachers of English (NCTE). (2016). Professional knowledge for the teacher of writing. Retrieved from http://www.ncte.org/positions/statements/teaching-writing

Ntelioglou, B. Y, Fannin, J., Montanera, M., & Cummins, J. (2014). A multilingual and multi-modal approach to literacy teaching and learning in urban education: A collaborative inquiry project in an urban inner city elementary school. *Frontiers in Psychology, 5*(533), 1–23.

Ray, K. W., & Laminack, L. L. (2001). Understanding the essential characteristics of the writing workshop. In K. W. Ray and L. L. Laminack (Eds.), *Writing workshop: The working through the hard parts (and they're all hard parts)* (pp. 1–15). Urbana, IL: NCTE.

Rowley, B. (1999). The good mentor. *Educational Leadership, 56*(8). Retrieved from http://www.ascd.org/publications/educational-leadership/may99/vol56/num08/The-Good-Mentor.aspx

Sandstrom, H., & Huerta, S. (2013). The negative effects of instability on child development: A research synthesis. Urban Institute: Low Income Working Families Discussion Paper 3. Retrieved from http://www.urban.org/sites/default/files/alfresco/publication-pdfs/412899-The-Negative-Effects-of-Instability-on-Child-Development-A-Research-Synthesis.PDF

Skerrett, A. & Bomer, R. (2011). Border zones in adolescent literacy practices: Connecting out-of-school literacies to the reading curriculum. *Urban Education, 46*, 1256–79.

Sokol, J. T. (2009). Identity development throughout the lifetime: An examination of the Eriksonian Theory. *Graduate Journal of Counseling Psychology, 1*(2), 1–10.

Strickland, D. S., Bodino, A., Buchan, M., Jones, K. M., Nelson, A., & Rosen, M. (2001). Teaching writing in a time of reform. *Elementary School Journal, 101*(4), 385–97.

Tschannen-Moran, M., & Woolfolk Hoy, A. (2007). The differential antecedents of self-efficacy beliefs of notice and experienced teachers. *Teaching and Teacher Education, 23*(6), 944–56.

Viel-Ruma, K., Houchins, D., Jolivette, K., & Benson, G. (2010). Efficacy beliefs among special educators: The relationship among collective efficacy, teacher self-efficacy, and job satisfaction. *Teacher Education and Special Education, 33*(3), 225–33.

Wang, J., & Odell, S. J. (2003). Learning to teach towards standards-based writing instruction: Experiences of two preservice teachers and two mentors in an urban, multicultural classroom. *Elementary School Journal, 104*(2), 147–74.

Winn, M. T., & Johnson, L. P. (2011). *Writing instruction in the culturally relevant classroom.* Urbana, IL: National Council for Teachers of English. Retrieved from https://secure.ncte.org/library/NCTEFiles/Resources/Books/Sample/58562Chap01_x.pdf

Woolfolk Hoy, A., & Burke Spero, R. (2005). Changes in teacher efficacy during the early years of teaching: A comparison of four measures. *Teaching and Teacher Education, 21*(4), 343–56.

Chapter Seven

Supporting Emergent Learners in Their Beginning Steps Toward Literacy

Margaret Thomson

Reading and writing in elementary grades rests on a firm foundation of emergent literacy skills. Oral language development, phonological awareness, book and print concepts, graphophonemic knowledge, understanding of the alphabetic principle, early decoding skills, instant recognition of high-frequency words, and development of emergent writing skills are the beginning steps on the road to full literary competency.

But for many diverse students in the nation's schools, cultural and learning differences complicate the process of acquiring these basic skills during the early years of schooling. Teachers must be aware of potential pitfalls, and be prepared to support students who struggle with literacy learning for a variety of reasons.

This chapter will review how emergent literacy skills such as oral language, phonological awareness, print concepts, graphophonemic knowledge, and high-frequency words support later reading fluency and comprehension skills, as well as proficiency in the craft and mechanics of writing.

ORAL LANGUAGE

It is easy to believe that literacy development doesn't begin until preschool and kindergarten as children learn the alphabet and its associated sounds or phonemes. However, according to Patricia Kuhl, codirector of the Institute for Learning & Brain Sciences at the University of Washington, literacy begins long before then—while a child is still in the womb. The vowel sounds in the mother's speech are the loudest units, and the fetus learns to recognize them (Moon, Lagercrantz, & Kuhl, 2013).

Newborns already prefer the cadence and phonology of their parents' native language over other languages. Babies are on the road to learning their first language long before they are born (Kisilevsky et al., 2003). In the first year of life, children continue to be active listeners, absorbing and practicing the sounds of language. Parents and caregivers help babies learn these sounds when they use exaggerated, high-pitched, slow, sing-song language known as "motherese" as they hold their babies and talk to them: "Look at the baby's toes!" Motherese allows babies to hear the sounds of language and connect words with their meaning. Babies babble, producing sounds that increasingly approximate the sounds of language (Ramirez-Esparza, Garcia-Sierra, & Kuhl, 2017).

At six months of age the child's echolalia, or wordlike babbling, typically mirrors the sounds of his home language, and linguists who listen to a recording of his babbling can determine his native language by analyzing the particular set of phonemes he is producing (Poulin-Dubois & Goodz, 2001). Through listening, the baby is developing his receptive vocabulary long before he can say anything. Throughout life his receptive vocabulary will be much larger than his expressive vocabulary.

At approximately one year of age, a child begins to say his first words. Known as "holographic speech," these one-word utterances are typically nouns and verbs. When he has about fifty words in his spoken vocabulary, he begins to use two-word, then three-word phrases known as "telegraphic speech." These short utterances have only the most meaningful words in them such as, "all gone" or "fall down." He is still refining his ability to pronounce sounds and adults who are not his parents or caregivers will have difficulty understanding him because many of his consonant sounds are still not clear.

A remarkable phenomenon known as the language explosion occurs during a child's second year. He begins to learn new words very quickly through a process known as "fast mapping." He is able learn a new word after hearing it as little as one time. By his second birthday, his expressive vocabulary will include several hundred words, and his receptive vocabulary will include thousands of words.

Halliday (2004) found that because children in early childhood are primarily egocentric, they use language to communicate about what is important to them. For example, a child will use language to ask for something she wants to eat, to learn more about something she sees or hears, to tell others what has happened to her, and to narrate her imaginative play.

Adults who interact with children by responding, mirroring, and extending what they say help children become increasingly adept language learners. By the time a child is old enough for kindergarten, she normally has mastered all the basic grammatical structures of her first language and is a competent communicator of all she knows.

The importance of early language learning cannot be underestimated. Much of the struggle that many second language learners have with reading and writing in their second language can be credited to their limited vocabulary and weak understanding of the grammatical structure of that language. Early support as children learn the language of school is critical. Teaching children to read and write in their first language, and supporting transfer of first language literacy to developing second language literacy, are both effective and affirming.

In their landmark study released in 1995, *Meaningful Differences in Everyday Experience of Young American Children*, Betty Hart and Todd Risley looked at the differences in linguistic development and academic progress among children from different socioeconomic backgrounds. Children from poverty had less than one-third as much experience with listening and speaking as the typical child whose parents were in the professional class. While a child from the professional class heard approximately eleven million words a year, the child from poverty heard only about three million words.

Parents of upper- and middle-class children tend to be much more verbal, engaging in extended conversations with their children even while they are still babies too young to respond. Parents from lower-class backgrounds interact with their children almost as frequently, but the interactions are shorter and more directive.

As a result, a child from a lower income family is far more likely to enter school with a significantly smaller vocabulary than a child from a higher income household. A more recent study found that 65 percent of low socioeconomic status preschoolers in Head Start programs had clinically significant language delays (Nelson, Welsh, Vance Trup, & Greenberg, 2011).

Because it is difficult to read and comprehend text full of words that are not already in the vocabulary of the reader, vocabulary knowledge is a strong predictor of future reading achievement. Teachers of students who are likely to have language delays, such as second language learners and children from poverty, should do everything possible to develop the oral language of their students by planning activities that strengthen and build all oral language skills, particularly vocabulary.

Teachers can encourage the growth of oral language by increasing the amount of interaction and discussion taking place in the classroom. Activities such as think-turn-talk, small-group interaction in learning centers, and paired reading of picture books engage children in meaningful discussions as they learn. Teachers must also make time for frequent verbal interaction with students during individual and small-group activities.

Reading Aloud

Because children's trade books are full of new vocabulary, reading aloud to children and having them reread with a partner or independently not only increases the quantity of new words that the child is encountering, but the quality as well. Children's literature is a rich source of new vocabulary for young children. It is far more sophisticated and complex than even the spoken language of college-educated adults (Trelease, 1982). The more children read and are read to from a variety of text genres, the more their receptive and expressive vocabulary will grow and, as a result, their reading comprehension will increase (Krashen, 2004).

Teachers should plan for several interactive read-aloud experiences each day, during which they read carefully selected texts from a variety of genres. Stopping strategically to engage students in a short discussion of key understandings or to discuss important features of the text builds language and understanding of these texts.

Effective teachers make the books used in read-alouds available in their classroom library and plan time every day for independent and paired reading, and encourage parents to read to their children every day (Cunningham & Zibulsky, 2014). In the landmark report titled *Becoming a Nation of Readers*, the federally funded Commission on Reading stated: "The single most important activity for building the knowledge required for eventual success is reading aloud to children" (Anderson, 1985, p. 247).

PHONOLOGICAL AWARENESS

Phonological awareness refers to a child's growing understanding of the sound units of oral language—words, syllables, onsets and rimes, and phonemes—and the child's ability to manipulate them. It does not include any letters or reading of text, but is strictly related to hearing and playing with sounds. Children who have phonological awareness can identify words they hear that have alliteration—the same initial sound, such as bat and ball—and words that rhyme because they have the same ending sounds, such as cat and fat.

Two- and three-year-olds enjoy hearing books, nursery rhymes, and songs that include these elements. They will join in, anticipating and supplying the rhyming word. This skill typically develops by the time a child leaves pre-K and enters kindergarten.

Children in kindergarten (or even younger) begin to understand that the continuous stream of sound that is spoken language can be broken into individual words. They develop the ability to segment sentences into words, and can count the words in a phrase or sentence that they hear. They also learn that bigger words can be divided into smaller units of sound called "syllables." They learn to orally segment words into syllables and blend syllables into words.

These abilities are critical for future reading and spelling success when written language is required. Children who cannot identify and manipulate sounds within spoken words have difficulty with the sound-to-print relationships necessary to encode or spell and decode or read words.

By first grade, a child is learning to separate the onset of a syllable from the rime. The onset of a syllable is the consonant phoneme or phonemes that are located at the beginning of a syllable before the vowel. The "rime" is the vowel phoneme and any consonant phonemes that may come after it in the syllable.

While all syllables have a rime, not all syllables, for example "at," have an onset. Being able to verbally segment a one-syllable word into its onset and rime and manipulate the sounds by substituting a different onset prepares the child to read and spell words that share the same rime in a word family, such as cat, hat, rat, fat, mat, chat, and even splat.

The final and most important level of phonological awareness for reading and spelling is phonemic awareness. Phonemic awareness is the ability to blend, segment, and manipulate individual phonemes, or sounds, in a word or syllable. When phonemes are manipulated, they can be deleted, new phonemes can be added or substituted, or the order of phonemes in the word can be changed. For example, "tip" becomes "top," "top" becomes "stop," and "stop" can become "pots." Phoneme manipulation is the most difficult of all phonological awareness skills.

Because of the strong relationship between phonological awareness—particularly phonemic awareness—and future reading and spelling, researchers can predict with a high level of accuracy whether a student will be a good or poor reader by the end of third grade by measuring phonological awareness at a much younger age (Houston & Torgesen, 2004).

Languages such as English, French, and Spanish use an alphabetic writing system in which "graphemes," or letters and letter combinations, represent individual phonemes. When a child can separate an unknown written word into its graphemes, recognize the phonemes represented by each grapheme, and blend the phonemes back together to read the word, the child is successfully using the alphabetic principle to get meaning from text (Troia & Graham, 2004).

Instruction that fosters phonological awareness, particularly at the onset-rime and phonemic awareness levels, should be incorporated into instruction every day in preschool, kindergarten, and first-grade classrooms. This can be accomplished through joyful, developmentally appropriate games and activities that build on young children's natural desire to experiment and play with the sounds of language.

English language learners may have difficulty with some aspects of phonological awareness in English. The difficulty lies in the mismatch between the set of phonemes learned in infancy and toddlerhood in their native language, and the different phonemes of the English language. For example, Spanish has twenty-four phonemes, five vowel sounds, and nineteen consonant sounds, while English has forty-four phonemes, twenty-six vowel sounds, and eighteen consonant sounds.

When a child is still in the process of learning English and its phonemes as a second language, she may not have developed the ability to distinguish between similar English phonemes that are not present in her first language. This can also be true for students who speak dialects of English that vary from the standard forty-four phonemes. Teachers of English language learners must be aware of the phonemic differences between a child's first and second languages, and be ready to bridge the gap with appropriate instruction for these students.

Children with dyslexia may have difficulty learning to read and spell due to a deficit in the phonological component of language that is "often unexpected in relation to other cognitive abilities and the provision of effective classroom instruction" (Lyon, Shaywitz, & Shaywitz, 2003, p. 2). Even when a dyslexic child receives direct instruction in phonological awareness, he is likely to have trouble with this skill (Gillon, 2017).

Learning difficulties related to the various phonological awareness skills is often the instructional "red flag" that leads to the diagnosis of dyslexia. With intensive, explicit, and targeted instruction, most dyslexic children can master phonological awareness. The close relationship between phonological awareness and future literacy means that every child's development of phonological awareness should be closely monitored so that he can receive immediate, appropriate instruction at the first sign of falling behind.

PRINT CONCEPTS

Another important component of early literacy learning is a child's understanding of the concepts related to print, how it is used, and how it works. Elizabeth Sulzby's (1985) research in this area focused on the stages of emergent storybook reading.

Infants and very young children are interested in books before they ever have the concept of what a story is. A child will look at the pictures and point at what interests him. As language develops, he will talk about what he sees in the pictures with no connection from page to page with the story. After hearing many stories, he may make up a story that goes with the pictures in the book, but is not necessarily the story that is in the book. However, as the child listens to a favorite storybook over and over, he begins to memorize the text and will "read" it, repeating the memorized words and inflection he has heard.

During this "pretend reading" stage, he is still attending to the pictures rather than to any text on the page, but the child appears to be reading. As the child matures, he begins to understand that the words of the story are recorded in the print rather than in the pictures. When he understands that decoding the print is how a reader knows what the book says, he may stop "reading" books and say he doesn't know how to read.

In the final stage of this progression, he learns to decode and returns to favorite texts, this time focusing on the print and trying to actually read what it says. These stages of development in which the child moves from attending to the pictures to attending to print reflect the child's growing understanding of what print is and how it works (Sulzby, 1985).

Children whose parents or caregivers read to them frequently pick up book concepts, such as knowing what the cover and title of a book are, what an author and illustrator are, how to hold a book and turn the pages and, eventually, knowing that the message of the book is in the print rather than in the text.

As they learn to read, children learn print concepts showing that they know where to start reading on a new page, that reading English goes from left to right and top to bottom on each page, that punctuation is important, and even that the space between words is there to show when one word ends and the next begins.

Children from other countries may need some direct instruction to learn the print concepts related to English, because the print in their country of origin may "work" in a different way. For example, Chinese and Japanese print materials are traditionally read from top to bottom and right to left.

Teachers can demonstrate how print works, model expressive reading of text, and promote the enjoyment of reading with shared reading as an essential part of each day's literacy instruction. In shared reading, a text that is large enough for all the students to see is turned toward the audience as the teacher reads aloud. Pointers are often used to help children track print from left to right as it is read.

Children are invited to join in when they reach familiar parts of the text. Shared reading supports children as they move from only being a listener toward becoming a participant in the reading process.

Print is a useful tool in getting things done! Its functions, or uses, include entertainment and enjoyment, providing information to help solve problems, and communicating information or directions to others. Children who come from homes with very few books, or where the adults are illiterate or alliterate, may have limited opportunities to develop this basic understanding about print (Cox & Thomson, 2006).

Teachers should explicitly point out the uses, or functions, of print in their "think-alouds" as they read and write with children. Understanding how print works and appreciating how it can be used to make our lives easier helps build a strong foundation for reading and writing in authentic contexts.

GRAPHOPHONEMIC KNOWLEDGE AND THE ALPHABETIC PRINCIPLE

Young children who have developed a strong literacy foundation in speaking and listening, who have a growing awareness of the sounds of their first language and have begun to master concepts of print, are ready for the next level of literacy development—reading and writing of text. Children as young as two years old notice letters in environmental print. Young children are particularly interested in the letters (particularly the first letter) found in their own names and those of their friends.

Graphophonemic knowledge involves a variety of skills, the most obvious of which is learning the phonemes associated with each letter or letter combination. Children must also learn to discriminate between letters with similar shapes, to recognize both upper and lower case for each letter, and eventually to recognize the same letter in various fonts.

After a few common or high-utility consonants are learned, the short sound of one or two vowels is taught. If a child has learned /l/, /m/, /p/, /t/, and /a/, she can begin to use the letters to spell words such as tap, mat, pat, pal, and even lamp.

Children should also have opportunities to practice reading in decodable texts that contain words that they are learning. Spelling and reading words with familiar letter-sound relationships helps a child learn about the predictable relationship between sounds and letters and how to apply this to familiar and unfamiliar words to decode, or read them (Cunningham & Allington, 2016). This understanding and application of the alphabetic principle is an important step forward toward literacy.

In the early stages of reading decodable texts, children learn the most common patterns for consonants and vowels in single-syllable words, and which vowel sounds (short, long, r-controlled, and diphthongs) are represented by each pattern. Knowledge of consonant digraphs and blends, and the less common sounds for some of the consonants, are next.

As children read and write, they are learning to self-monitor, asking themselves if what they read makes sense, looks right, and sounds right. By the end of first grade, a skillful young reader is moving from letter-to-letter reading toward recognizing familiar "chunks" or patterns in new words, reading them by analogy, and applying known patterns to figure out new words (Duke & Block, 2012).

HIGH-FREQUENCY WORDS

Of the hundreds of thousands of words in the English language, a very small number make up much of what is actually read. These are called "high-frequency words." The thirteen most common words (e.g., the, to, and, he, a, I, and you) make up 25 percent of what we read. The one hundred most frequent words make up 50 percent of the words on a typical page.

Many of these words are irregular. They don't follow the commonly taught patterns of phonics, and can't be sounded out. They must be memorized in order to be recognized instantly when encountered in text. It is a great advantage to the reader to recognize all high-frequency words instantly as a whole rather than having to pause and attempt to figure out most of the words on a page. Instant recognition means that high-frequency words are now sight words for the reader. If most words on the page are sight words, the result is a faster and more fluent reader.

Comprehension of the text increases as the memory is not overloaded with the task of figuring out every word. High frequency words are introduced and taught as whole units rather than by sounding them out. For struggling and dyslexic readers, more repetitions for each word will likely be necessary, but the increased and intensive practice to master at least the first one hundred high-frequency words is an important step toward reading fluency.

READING COMPREHENSION

Children should have the opportunity to apply their growing mastery of sight words and decoding as they read in both authentic and leveled texts, and to utilize the words in their daily writing activities. Culturally relevant texts support children by helping the reader connect text with his own life and experiences and building reading comprehension abilities. This is particularly true for bilingual children who are being instructed in English.

When students can connect with a text on many levels, they read better and more (Freeman & Freeman, 2014). What makes a text culturally relevant? The closer the characters are in the text to the reader's age, gender, language, culture and family structure, the easier it is for the reader to understand and relate to the text. Colorín Colorado's website (http://www.colorincolorado.org/) offers an extensive list of high-quality, culturally relevant books with helpful reviews.

Some examples are *Too Many Tamales* by Gary Soto, *I Love Saturdays y domingos* by Alma Flor Ada, *Meet Danitra Brown* by Nikki Grimes, and *Lift Ev'ry Voice and Sing* by James Weldon Johnson.

All children should have the opportunity to learn about the world as they read both widely and deeply from a variety of authors and genres. But when reading is difficult or motivation is low, culturally relevant elements in books offer a scaffold as children build both stamina and a love of reading that supports them as they learn to read and write.

EMERGENT WRITING

Emergent writing begins when young children "begin to understand that writing is a form of communication and their marks on paper convey a message" (Mayer, 2007, p. 2). Reading and writing develop simultaneously and have a reciprocal relationship in which the better a child becomes at writing, the better he is at reading. The better he is at reading, the better he becomes at writing (Puranik, Lonigan, & Kim, 2011).

There is a predictable continuum of writing development. It begins with a very young preliterate child's scribbling and drawing, progresses to letter-like forms that look more like letters, then moves to letter strings that are actual letters, except that the string doesn't phonetically represent real words.

As children begin to grasp the alphabetic principle, they use invented spelling with, at first, the initial sound represented by the correct letter, and later with ending and then middle sounds represented by a letter or letters that spell the sounds. Eventually, spelling will be conventional, with all or almost all of the sounds in a word represented with the correct graphemes. Each of the steps parallels the child's progress in other areas of literacy, such as print concepts, graphophonemic knowledge, and understanding of the alphabetic principle.

Teachers, caregivers, and parents of emergent writers should accept all developmentally appropriate levels of writing while holding the student responsible for skills already mastered. A student's writing errors should be seen as an opportunity to understand what he is "using but confusing." This knowledge helps teachers understand what needs to be modeled and taught during shared or interactive writing lessons.

In a shared writing experience, the teacher models writing for a group of students, recording what they say. As the teacher writes what the students dictate on a large surface such as chart paper, concepts of print, graphophonemic knowledge, and the alphabetic principle are demonstrated. "Think-alouds" are used to make what the teacher is thinking and the decisions about spelling, punctuation, capitalization, and syntax clear to students.

Writer's workshop is a daily time dedicated to writing. The workshop consists of a short writing mini-lesson, an extended time for student writing and teacher/student conferences, followed by a time to share writing. An important opportunity to teach the writing skills most needed by students occurs when teachers use their observations during a writer's workshop to plan mini-lessons based on examples from the children's own writing.

These observations make the mini-lesson very pertinent to the children's needs and provide a "teachable moment" for instruction. The writing and conferring time gives students the opportunity to write independently every day with the support of a nearby adult. Daily sharing time helps create a community of writers who celebrate each other's writing successes. Writer's workshop helps students see themselves as writers as well as readers.

Learning centers with embedded writing opportunities support emergent writing throughout the day. Every classroom should have a library center to provides access to books that can serve as mentor texts for writing.

A classroom writing center is another "must" for emergent readers and writers. It should be well stocked with materials such as a variety of paper, envelopes, post-it notes, a date stamp, blank books, clipboards, and a variety of writing tools. Anchor charts that remind children of key ideas from writing mini-lessons and prompts for what to write about should be in the writing center.

A picture dictionary, a word wall, and a chart with names of classmates all support authentic writing. Imaginative play in dramatic play centers can also provide rich opportunities for using writing in practical ways. A "waiter" in the "restaurant" can write down the food order for a "customer"; a "dad" can write a "to do" or "shopping list." A "plumber" can create a "bill" for his services.

Independent writing activities for emergent writers should focus on writing for authentic purposes rather than writing to prompts and similar assignments. Allowing children to choose what they will write about and to write about what is personally important builds a love of writing and an understanding of its real-life uses. In print-rich environments where young children hear stories and engage in imaginative play, an atmosphere for growth in both authentic reading and writing is fostered (Neuman & Roskos, 2007).

FINAL THOUGHTS

This chapter examined the emergent literacy skills on which rest later literacy skills, such as fluency and comprehension in reading and proficiency in both the mechanics and craft of writing. Support strategies for struggling readers and writers were shared.

Because literacy is the key to future academic and career success for all students, teachers and administrators must be fully prepared to help each one reach full proficiency. Educators who are well informed concerning the particular learning challenges and diverse backgrounds of their students can be proactive in their instruction, providing equity and support on the road to fully developed literacy for all their students.

REFERENCES

Ada, A. F. (2002). *I love Saturdays y domingos.* New York: Aladdin Paperbacks.

Anderson, R. C. (1985). *Becoming a nation of readers: the report of the Commission on Reading.* Pittsburgh, PA: National Academy of Education.

Cox, L., & Thomson, M. (2006). Helping struggling authors leap the barriers to authentic writing. Lecture presented at Texas State Reading Association, Austin, Texas.

Cunningham, P. M., & Allington, R. L. (2016). *Classrooms that work they can all read and write.* Boston: Pearson.

Cunningham, A. E., & Zibulsky, J. (2014). *Book smart: how to develop and support successful, motivated readers.* New York: Oxford University Press.

Duke, N. K., & Block, M. K. (2012). Improving reading in the primary grades. *The Future of Children, 22*(2), 55–72.

Freeman, D. E., & Freeman, Y. S. (2014). *Essential linguistics: What teachers need to know to teach ESL, reading, spelling, grammar.* Portsmouth, NH: Heinemann.

Gillon, G. T. (2017). *Phonological awareness: From research to practice.* New York: Guilford Press.

Grimes, N. (1997). *Meet Danitra Brown.* New York: Harper Collins.

Halliday, M. A. K. (2004). *The language of early childhood.* London: Continuum.

Hart, B., & Risley, T. R. (1995). *Meaningful differences in the everyday experience of young American children.* Baltimore, MD: Paul H. Brookes.

Houston, D., & Torgesen, J. (2004). *Teaching students with moderate disabilities to read: Insights from research.* Tallahassee: Bureau of Instructional Support and Community Services, Florida Department of Education.

Johnson, J. W. (1995). *Lift ev'ry voice and sing.* New York: Scholastic.

Kisilevsky, B. S., Hains, S. M., Lee, K., Xie, X., Huang, H., Ye, H. H., & Wang, Z. (2003). Effects of experience on fetal voice recognition. *Psychological Science, 14*(3), 220–24.

Krashen, S. D. (2004). *The power of reading: Insights from the research.* Westport, CT: Libraries Unlimited.

Lyon, G. R., Shaywitz, S. E., & Shaywitz, B. A. (2003). A definition of dyslexia. *Annals of Dyslexia, 53*(1), 1–14.

Mayer, K. (2007). Research in review: Emerging knowledge about emergent writing. *Young Children, 62*(1), 34–40.

Moon, C., Lagercrantz, H., & Kuhl, P. (2013). Language experienced in utero affects vowel perception after birth: A two-country study. *Acta Paediatrica, 102*(2), 156–60.

Nelson, K. E., Welsh, J. A., Vance Trup, E. M., & Greenberg, M. T. (2011). Language delays of impoverished preschool children in relation to early academic and emotion recognition skills. *First Language , 31 ,* 164–94.

Neuman, S. B., & Roskos, K. (2007). *Nurturing knowledge: Building a foundation for school success by linking early literacy to math, science, art, and social studies.* New York: Scholastic.

Poulin-Dubois, D., & Goodz, N. (2001). Language differentiation in bilingual infants: Evidence from babbling. In J. Cenoz & F. Genesee (Eds.), *Trends in bilingual acquisition research* (pp. 95–106). Amsterdam: John Benjamins.

Puranik, C. S., Lonigan, C. J., & Kim, Y. (2011). Contributions of emergent literacy skills to name writing, letter writing, and spelling in preschool. *Early Childhood Research Quarterly, 26*(4), 465–74.

Ramirez-Esparza, N., Garcia-Sierra, A., & Kuhl, P. (2017). Look who's talking now! Parentese, speech, social context and language development across time. *Frontiers in Psychology,* June 27. doi:10.3389/fpsyg.2017.01008

Soto, G. (1993). *Too many tamales.* New York: Putnam and Grosset Group.

Sulzby, E. (1985). Children's emergent reading of favorite storybooks: A developmental study. *Reading Research Quarterly, 20*(4), 458–81.

Trelease, J. (1982). *The new read-aloud handbook.* New York: Penguin Books.

Troia, G. A., & Graham, S. (2004). *Students who are exceptional and writing disabilities: Prevention, practice, intervention, and assessment.* Mahwah, NJ: Lawrence Erlbaum Associates.

Chapter Eight

Engaging Beginning Readers and Writers in Visual Literacy through Picture Books

Jacqueline Easley

Children's picture books constitute a unique genre of children's literature because they are defined by their format rather than their content. The format of a picture book is one of codependency: the written word conveys meaning to the reader, but it depends on the illustrations to convey additional (sometimes more) information not contained in the words. Barbara Cooney (1988) captured this genre's codependency of words and pictures when she equated a picture book to a string of pearls: the words are the strings, and the pictures, the pearls.

Picture books are used widely in primary-level classrooms. Teachers integrate them into all subjects, read them aloud to set a purpose for learning new content, and maintain them in classroom libraries for their students' use during independent reading time. While many teachers guide their students in using the illustrations to make predictions or draw conclusions, they should also discuss with the class the illustrator's intentional use of visual elements, such as line, color, shape, texture, and composition, to convey more nuanced information to the reader. In this way, teachers engage their readers in the practice of visual literacy.

When readers focus on visual literacy, they develop inferential and critical thinking skills as they interpret and analyze picture book illustrations. Furthermore, teachers should foster interactive discussions about the emotions, social issues, and cultural values conveyed through the illustrations.

This involves perceiving themselves as "co-constructor[s] of knowledge" because they situate themselves with their students, interacting with the picture book to construct their comprehension through both the words and the illustrations (Hassett & Curwood, 2009, p. 280). When readers consider these elements and concepts while thinking about the text, they begin to develop their visual literacy: "the ability to find meaning in imagery" (Yenawine, 1997, p. 845).

The purpose of this chapter is to describe how visual elements are used as tools by picture book illustrators to convey emotions, information, and cultural experiences. Furthermore, this chapter will engage its readers in an exploration of social justice activities in response to culturally specific picture books. The exploration of illustrators' uses of the visual elements of line, shape, color, texture, and composition will be accomplished by examining these elements in Christian Robinson's award-winning illustrations for *Last Stop on Market Street* by Matt de la Peña (2015). This book will serve as a template that will allow teachers to apply their knowledge of visual elements to their reading of other culturally specific picture books to their students.

The chapter concludes with a resource table listing additional culturally responsive and specific picture books, along with the social issues and visual elements that dominate each book's content/illustrations.

READERS' TRANSACTIONS WITH THE ILLUSTRATIONS

According to Louise Rosenblatt's (1994; 1995) transactional theory of literature, readers interact with the author, the illustrator, and the text to actively construct meaning. As a beginning reader takes in both the written and visual text of a picture book, she is actively engaged in blending personal experiences (such as cultural, social, emotional, and physical connections) to the content of the literary work.

The beginning reader is receiving the written text in a linear process (we read text from left to right), while being immersed in the visual text all at once, without direction or guidance. This reader-text-author-illustrator transaction occurs with each turn of the page. Thus, the beginning reader subconsciously assimilates her personal experiences onto the visual text, directing her attention toward some objects, while neglecting others.

As the beginning reader transacts with these two texts (written and visual), she "adopts a selective attitude or stance, bringing certain aspects into the center of attention and pushing others into the fringes of consciousness" (Rosenblatt, 1994, p. 1066). In other words, readers generally position their minds on a continuum of purpose between a primarily efferent stance, in which the purpose is to understand and retain information, and a primarily aesthetic stance, wherein the purpose is to interpret ideas, feelings, and moods.

Typically, beginning readers are instructed to focus on developing the correct interpretations of a text—an efferent stance. This occurs through the teacher's use of questions that evoke the reader's recollection of facts and details. These are important skills for reading, to be sure. However, it is also important for teachers to intentionally nurture beginning readers' abilities to interpret moods, feelings, and personal connections to literature by teaching them to develop an aesthetic stance. In doing so, beginning readers will see reading as more than a way to gain information, but rather as a way to personally connect to text by constructing new ideas, challenging mind-sets, and creatively thinking about the illustrator's artistic representation of the text.

Teachers can develop the aesthetic stance in their readers by asking questions before and during the reading of the book that encourage creative responses, discussion, and personal connections, such as:

- Look at the cover of the book. What do you notice about the colors the illustrator has used here?
- Does the title remind you of a similar experience you've had?
- Why do you suppose the illustrator included _____ in the illustration?
- How do you feel about the main character? What did the illustrator do to make you feel this way?
- What are you curious about? How did the illustrator raise your curiosity about this in the cover illustration?

After reading a book, teachers can encourage students to aesthetically respond through various drawing and writing activities. Rather than simply assigning students to "write a paragraph about . . ." or "draw a picture of your favorite character," teachers can delve into creative responses and authentic activities with prompts along the efferent–aesthetic continuum. See table 8.1 for suggested activities that encompass the efferent–aesthetic continuum.

EXPLORING VISUAL LITERACY THROUGH *LAST STOP ON MARKET STREET*

In today's diverse classrooms, teachers can best serve the needs of their beginning readers by sharing culturally specific picture books (Hollie, 2011). Such books convey responsive and authentic experiences based on culture rather than race. They "help children understand who they are and become confident that their experiences matter" (Fleming, Catapano, Thompson, & Ruvalcaba Carrillo, 2016, p. 62).

How can teachers engage their beginning readers in thinking critically about the illustrations in culturally responsive picture books? In what ways can teachers foster their students' visual literacy through creative writing activities?

Table 8.1. **Drawing and Writing Activities along the Efferent–Aesthetic Continuum**

Activity	Efferent	Efferent–Aesthetic	Aesthetic–Efferent	Aesthetic
Drawing	Draw: a main character setting of . . . main idea/ theme of . . .	Use the illustrator's artistic technique to create your favorite scene.	Use the illustrator's artistic technique to create a new adventure for the main character.	Explore the illustrator's artistic techniques to create a picture of a similar experience you've had in your life.
Writing	Write: a summary of . . . a description of . . . the sequence of events of . . .	Write a letter to the main character's friend about a problem in the story.	Write a song or poem about the main character's accomplishment in the story.	How does this story make you feel about ____? Write a letter to ____ to tell him/her about your feelings and suggest ideas to improve the situation/issue.

The illustrations by Christian Robinson in *Last Stop on Market Street* (de la Peña, 2015), winner of the 2016 Newbery Award as well as the Caldecott Honor Award and Coretta Scott King Honor Award, will be used to explore these questions. This seminal picture book is culturally specific (Hollie, 2011) because it "illuminate[s] the authentic experience of growing up as a member of a particular cultural group" (p. 86).

Perkins (2009) encouraged teachers to ask themselves several key questions when evaluating the "cultural accuracy" (Gay, 2010, p. 141) of a book. These include the ways that race and ethnicity are portrayed, noting how literary characters act as change agents, and the realistic portrayal of the characters in the illustrations. Given the critical acclaim and cultural accuracy of de la Peña's picture book, *Last Stop on Market Street* (hereafter referred to as *Market Street*) will serve as an excellent template upon which to discuss visual literacy and to empower teachers to engage their students in exploring their thinking about illustrations through spoken and written discourse.

One way in which teachers could demonstrate an aesthetic stance in reading the illustrations is to lead the students in a critical examination of Robinson's use of character position in the cover illustration to convey emotions and/or psychological realities (Schwarcz & Schwarcz, 1991). On the cover of the book, the main character, CJ, stands at the center and holds his nana's hand. She is near the right side of the illustration, and both of their heads are turned to face the left side of the page as the bus approaches their stop. Robinson's placement of the two main characters seems to block the natural progression of the story (we turn pages from right to left).

This subtle placement of CJ and his nana, blocking the forward progress of turning the page in the book, seems to suggest CJ's initial negative attitude toward taking the bus down Market Street. Meanwhile, the bus is facing the right side of the cover, subtly encouraging the reader to open the book and turn the page to see what will happen on Market Street.

So, let's open the book and join CJ and his nana on their journey, while looking closely at Robinson's use of visual elements and cultural artifacts to convey feelings and moods, and add depth to de la Peña's story line.

Visual Elements: Line and Shape

Illustrators convey feelings depending on the shape, direction, and thickness of lines. Rounded shapes tend to imply a sense of softness. They are associated with nature and portray an organic, calm feeling to the reader (Nodelman, 1996). Throughout *Market Street*, Robinson portrays characters with spherical heads (as opposed to angular jaw lines, for instance), rounded shoulders, and circular bends in their arms, all of which reinforce the calm, natural love between CJ and his nana, and between his nana and the people in their community. Even the corners of the bus are rounded rather than angular.

When illustrators create diagonal lines, they typical do so to convey a sense of anxiety. Alternately, horizontal and vertical lines convey stability and safety (Kiefer, 1995). So, as the reader begins the journey along Market Street on the book's dedication page, she encounters a double-spread illustration of Market Street in which Robinson uses progressively diagonal lines that move from the lower left toward the upper right.

The buildings, however, consist of horizontal and vertical lines, with a lone tree, in full, circular bloom, near the center of the street. Therefore, while the story will proceed with a gently conveyed uphill climb toward the problem of CJ's reluctance to ride the bus along Market Street, the reader is subconsciously reassured that this problem will not be insurmountable, and that Market Street is located in a loving, safe community.

This message is reinforced on the next page, where the story begins. Here, Robinson zooms in on a few buildings on Market Street. Globular, organic shapes dominate the scene, with rounded doorways, umbrellas, and church windows. The tree now takes center stage with its large, green biomorphic shape demanding the reader's attention. Here, too, the reader will notice that

CJ is the only character with his arms extended diagonally away from his body: Robinson wants him to stand out.

When teaching the element of line, it will be effective to use kinesthetic experiences with beginning readers. First, have the students stand beside their desks and extend one arm out from their body so that it is parallel to the floor. Next, direct the students to place a pencil or crayon on their extended arm and ask, "Do you feel confident that your pencil will stay on your arm?" They should answer affirmatively.

Follow this by having students slowly lower their extended arms toward the floor, pausing to ask whether they feel anxious about their pencil remaining on their arms. Do this until their pencil slides down their arms and then have them return to their seats. Talk about the line of their arms and link their feelings to illustrations of lines in a picture book.

Connect their confidence when their arms were straight to the illustrator's use of a straight horizontal line to convey safety and security. Continue the lesson by showing the students an illustration of a diagonal line, and discuss how this illustration creates a sense of anxiety or uncertainty for the readers.

Visual Element: Color

Illustrators typically choose colors with intention. Is it an accident that CJ's shirt is bright yellow with red and blue accents? Given that these are the primary colors, the reader could speculate that Robinson was intentional in choosing them for his main/primary character. According to Kiefer (1995), "color is one of the most expressive elements" (p. 124). This element can imply emotions, cultural symbols, and personality. Bright colors, for example, tend to convey more intense feelings, while softer colors imply serenity. Other times, colors convey a sense of warmth and affection.

This is evident when we turn to the next page in *Market Street* to find that Robinson used the color red for Nana's large umbrella. The umbrella occupies a dominant position on the double-spread illustration. Its color is reflected in the puddle beneath CJ's and Nana's feet. Robinson brings their warm, loving relationship full circle, encompassing them as they venture out into the gray world around them.

On this same page, Robinson placed a white birch tree. As an American cultural symbol, white tends to stand for purity and honesty. This color is repeated in Nana's hair, CJ's shoes, and the rain drops, which fall at a slight diagonal to emphasize a steady, yet gentle, challenge to their journey. While the gray background might convey trepidation, the bright colors of the umbrella, CJ's clothing, and the green grass and leaves overpower the sense of dread and reinforce the emotions of warmth and love. Notice, too, that Nana and CJ are positioned facing the right—encouraging us to turn the page.

Throughout the book, Robinson uses background colors to express emotions. When the bus finally arrives, two pages later, Robinson's sky is a cheerful blue. Deeper blue hues accent the illustration, along with bright red, green, and yellow cars. Robinson's colors convey happiness, as CJ and Nana can look forward to a safe, joyful ride along the street. Here, the bus and street are on a downward angle toward the right side of the page, implying safety and shelter from the rainy weather. Once on the bus, Robinson continues to use bright colors and a soft green background.

One way to teach beginning readers about the various colors and their symbolism is to create a color wheel, similar to that used by art teachers, to demonstrate primary and secondary colors. For each color on the wheel, write a word describing the mood it often symbolizes. This is most effectively accomplished while sharing a picture book and examining the colors in the illustrations together, to lead the students in choosing the best words to describe the mood that a color is conveying. Once the teacher and students create this wheel together as a class, display it for reference as various picture books are read aloud throughout the school year.

According to Cooper (1978), the following moods are conveyed for each color:

1. Primary Colors:

- red = love, joy, passion (in both love and anger), energy, health, fire, sexuality (p. 40)
- blue = truth, intelligence, wisdom, chastity, peace, coolness (p. 40)
- yellow = intelligence, light of the sun, goodness; dark yellow = treachery, greed, betrayal (p. 42)

2. Secondary Colors:

- purple = royalty, truth, justice, pride (p. 41)
- green = youth, hope, jealousy, life (p. 40)
- orange = flame, luxury (p. 40)

3. Hues:

- black = darkness, death, despair, sadness (p. 39)
- white = purity, perfection, light, air, innocence, holy (p. 41)

Visual Element: Texture

An illustrator's ability to convey depth on a two-dimensional surface entails the creation of texture. Robinson's multimedia illustrations consist of acrylic paints and collage. Throughout the picture book, he overlaps paints and papers to add a third dimension to his characters and settings. He achieves this effect in his portrayal of the characters' clothing. Here, Robinson uses cut paper for the foundation of the clothing, and then applies patterns with acrylic paints. He also uses this technique for CJ's hair: he paints swirls of black over half of CJ's brown head to indicate dark, curly hair.

Later, when CJ and Nana arrive at their destination, the reader will notice Robinson's use of crosshatching to create fencing and security gates. This use of texture creates a contrast to the otherwise stable lines of the cityscape.

When teaching students to understand the illustrator's use of texture, it is helpful to begin by thinking aloud during the reading of a texture-rich picture book. For example, while reading *Market Street*, the teacher should pause after reading the text with the double-spread illustration of CJ, his eyes closed, his arms extended, seeing in his mind the "sunset colors swirling over crashing waves" (unnumbered page).

Before turning the page, say to the students:

> I see that Mr. Robinson took his time here [pointing to CJ's hair] with his picture of CJ. He made his hair have texture by painting black swirls. His head and hands were made with brown paper, but Mr. Robinson took the time to add texture by coloring over the paper with a brown crayon. I think he wants us to understand that CJ is a unique person. He made CJ three-dimensional with this added texture. Let's see if we can notice other ways in which Mr. Robinson created a three-dimensional effect by adding texture while we read this book.

Composition—The Unification of All Visual Elements

As CJ and Nana meet various passengers on the bus, the colorful clothing, organic shapes, and rounded lines continue to convey warmth, love, and familial bliss. Matt de la Peña writes, "The bus lurched forward and stopped, lurched forward and stopped. Nana hummed as she knit. 'How come we always gotta go here after church?' CJ said. 'Miguel and Colby never have to go nowhere'" (unnumbered page).

On this double-spread illustration, Robinson employs a gray-green background with large, white window openings for the text. Four characters occupy the bus seats: Nana, an older woman, and a tattooed bald man sit facing the reader while CJ's back is turned to look out the windows as he talks to his nana. Again, Robinson continues to use spherical shapes for heads and eyes, rounded shoulders and knees. The characters wear brightly colored clothes. The tattooed man has his arms crossed while looking at his cell phone. Each character's skin tone is different.

Perhaps Robinson is asking the reader to confront his stereotypes of how people expect others to behave. What assumptions do we make about the older woman holding a jar of white butterflies? What do we expect the tattooed man to do or say? These are questions that Robinson seems to ask of the reader. His use of rounded lines, combined with a horizontal flow across the page of characters sitting on the bus, suggest that each passenger is unique, yet innocuous.

Nana and CJ continue to smile, reinforcing the notion that they are not concerned for their safety on the bus, and therefore the reader should feel safe, too. Furthermore, although CJ clearly isn't yet convinced that this journey down Market Street is one he wants to take, his Nana will lovingly show him how to look beyond the surface and see the beauty of this journey, just like Robinson asks the reader to do in seeing beyond stereotypes.

As more people join the passengers along the bus route, CJ and Nana meet a blind man, teenage boys, and a man with a guitar. All along the story line, Robinson uses bright colors on their clothing, various skin tones, and a gray-green background color. The bright colors add a joyful contrast to the background, which reinforces CJ's evolution from unenthusiastic partaker to self-actualized participant.

The pivotal moment occurs when CJ listens to the guitar player's song. Matt de la Peña writes, "And in the darkness, the rhythm lifted CJ out of the bus, out of the busy city" (unnumbered page). Here, Robinson fills the background with a two-toned, deep-sea blue. He places a bright-yellow round sun in the upper-left corner, and a bright-orange ocular shape in the upper-right corner. The shape has yellow tissue-paper birds collaged over it.

Two white butterflies, depicting those found in the older woman's jar, hover overhead. CJ's profile, eyes closed and mouth grinning, occupies the center. A black ocular shape is added to his background. These bold colors emphasize CJ's transformation in his ability to see the beauty in his community by closing his eyes and feeling music envelope his senses. His brightly colored sweater of primary colors contributes to the double-spread illustration by underscoring the joy and warmth that surround CJ on the bus.

Furthermore, Robinson adds texture to CJ's skin tone by incorporating dark brown crayon strokes over monochromatic light brown paper cut out for his head and hands. Although Robinson used this texturizing technique in earlier illustrations of CJ, it is most visible here because CJ takes up the majority of the double-spread. This depth of color in his skin tone reinforces the depth of his transformation as a wholly three-dimensional character who learns to see beauty beneath the surface of common experiences.

SOCIAL/CULTURAL VALUES CONVEYED
IN THE ILLUSTRATIONS

How does Robinson convey his personal cultural experience through his illustrations in this picture book? As Kiefer (1995) notes, "[w]hen responding to picturebooks [sic], children must also discriminate and interpret what they see" (p. 8). In *Market Street*, children see an urban landscape, filled with diverse people and city life.

Schwarcz and Schwarcz (1991) observed, in their review of urban life depicted in picture books of the late twentieth century, that "the large majority of children will continue to grow up and spend their lives in cities; this means that the picture book should indeed be expected to encourage social awareness by giving expression to discontent and doubt as well as by offering opportunities to identify with efforts to improve the existing, predominantly urban social fabric" (p. 144). Beginning readers must be exposed to culturally specific picture books wherein they have the opportunity to engage in an aesthetic stance and explore the illustrator's portrayal of urban life.

Upon CJ and Nana's arrival at the last stop on Market Street, Matt de la Peña writes,

> CJ looked around as he stepped off the bus. Crumbling sidewalks and broken-down doors, graffiti-tagged windows and boarded-up stores. He reached for his Nana's hand. "How come it's always so dirty over here?" She smiled and pointed to the sky. "Sometimes when you're surrounded by dirt, CJ, you're a better witness for what's beautiful." (unnumbered page)

Christian Robinson's illustrations accompanying these words demonstrate both the reality of urban life as well as the beauty hidden in plain sight. Nana and CJ are small figures on the left side of the double spread, walking toward the right, following a man in a wheelchair who is following another man pushing a shopping cart filled with a variety of shapes/belongings. A flock of black, gray, and white pigeons lift off in flight, gradually flying toward the upper right side of the illustration.

This slight diagonal is offset by the stable, strong vertical lines of the city buildings. The center building, colored burnt orange with blue-green windows stamped across the front, has yellow graffiti across it that reads, outlined in blue, "ONE LOVE," the "O" in "love" shaped as a heart. Beauty hidden in plain sight.

Upon turning the page, Robinson zooms out the reader's perspective so that the buildings are set back, and CJ and Nana are smaller. They have walked further down the street, continuing their progress across the double spread to the right, following the man in the wheelchair. The burnt-orange building is now located just left of center, and a rainbow spreads behind the building, flowing up so that, after reading "ONE LOVE," the reader's eye follows the arc of the rainbow as it extends behind a red brick building and arcs down behind a faded blue building; a few pigeons fly off the upper right corner of the page.

The rainbow's presence is a reminder of the beauty found in urban life, while the pigeons convey a sense of joy in their flight. Robinson's use of color, both bright and pastel, conveys a subtle, quiet joy. The sturdy lines and shapes of the buildings reinforce this feeling. Crosshatching along the base line represents fencing and building security gates. Their contrasting lines create balance, which adds to the stability and tranquility of the setting.

On the next page, Robinson positions the reader on the same eye level as Nana, CJ, and the community members in line for the soup kitchen. We, the readers/viewers, are one of the community members, taking our place in line. We join the diverse population portrayed in the illustration: various races, ages, genders; all of us. Here, CJ simply states, "'I'm glad we came'" (unnumbered page). The soft, pale-yellow walls and teal-blue window echo this sentiment, as do the round, smiling faces of the people in line and the thick, sturdy vertical lines of the gateway and shopping cart, along with the satisfying progression of the movement from left to right.

On the last page, Nana replies, "'Me too, CJ. Now come on'" (unnumbered page). Suddenly, the reader encounters a double-spread illustration of a bright, cheery blue background with white tables and colorful people eating and serving food. CJ, Nana, and another person each have white ovals on their heads, signifying hair nets (or halos?), as they serve food to smiling faces representing people from various cultures.

The reader's perspective is hovering overhead, the omniscient observer of the soup kitchen. Here, Robinson gives us the opportunity to pause and reflect, take in the rainbow of people that is present in this room, and say to ourselves, "Me, too!"

TAKING ACTION: AUTHENTIC SOCIAL JUSTICE ACTIVITIES

When reading books like *Last Stop on Market Street* (de la Peña, 2015), teachers should take the opportunity to discuss the illustrations as windows on social justice issues with their students.

Artistic Display

One such opportunity presents itself in a discussion of the bus passengers illustrated on the pages that read, "The bus lurched forward and stopped . . ." (unnumbered page). Here, as described earlier in this chapter, the reader faces four passengers: Nana, CJ, an older woman holding a jar of white butterflies, and a tattooed man looking at his cell phone. Robinson has positioned us (the readers) as if we are sitting across the aisle from these passengers. We are at eye level, looking at them as if confronting our stereotypes of people of different races, ages, and physical appearances.

A powerful response activity to this double-spread illustration involves a personalized art project. First, have students think about several people from their communities and/or families that might look different, but are very similar in their desires to live happy, healthy lives. Provide a sheet of light-green construction paper to serve as the inside of the bus, and guide the students in using patterned papers and crayons to create three or four collages of their own community/family members, looking straight ahead for all of us to see and reflect on.

Encourage the students to use bright colors to reflect cheerful moods, and diagonal lines if they want to show action. Discuss the differences that we can celebrate and the similarities in goals, dreams, personalities, ideas, talents, and other attributes. After the students share their artwork with the class, the teacher should hang them up in the hallway with the caption: "We are all different and we are all alike." Add words or phrases from the class discussion to illuminate elements of shared dreams.

Civic Literacy Project

Another social justice issue raised in this book, and several other picture books, is the need for soup kitchens. This is a significant issue in our society, and should be implemented as a civic literacy project (Epstein, 2014). The first step in such a project involves identifying the issue, which is accomplished here by discussing soup kitchens after reading this book. Next, the teacher will develop a way for the students to explore the issue by studying and writing about it.

Beginning readers should start by identifying soup kitchens' presence within their communities. The teacher could plan a field trip to the local soup kitchen and/or food pantry to connect the concept in a concrete way for their students. Upon return to the classroom, teachers could lead the class in a language experience activity. This involves having the students dictate to the teacher a retelling of their experience at the soup kitchen while the teacher writes their ideas on chart paper for everyone to see and reread together.

The final step in a civic literacy project involves taking action (Epstein, 2014). An authentic writing activity that would encourage students' understanding and participation in local food pantries and/or soup kitchens involves having students write letters to local businesses in which they first describe the positive impact of the local food pantry/soup kitchen, and then tell about the need for these service entities.

Students would then ask for donations of food and/or money to assist the mission of these service groups. By composing letters, students are writing for a real audience. They will take care to follow written conventions, use key vocabulary to fully describe the situation, and read the replies they will receive with intense motivation and purpose.

As the class receives replies from local businesses, the letters become authentic texts to develop their beginning reading skills. The teacher and students should set a goal for donations of money and/or food. As donations arrive, the class will keep track of money received by coloring in a drawing of a food item or other visual representation of their project. They could do the same for food donations.

Continue to take action in this project by having the students follow a recipe to make biscuits to donate to a local soup kitchen. This beginning reading activity provides authentic practice in developing word recognition skills while serving a higher purpose. After reading this type of picture book, discuss ways in which they could make a difference in providing food to people in their community who need support. Lead them to the conclusion that the class will make biscuits to donate to the local soup kitchen.

Provide small groups of students with the recipe (written using language that beginning readers can read and comprehend) and all the supplies. Lead the class step by step in following the recipe; then, as they clean up and begin their own silent reading time, take the biscuits into the school kitchen to bake (perhaps the school cooks and/or teacher aides can assist with watching the timer, and other chores). Once the biscuits are baked and cooled, bag them up and have the students write a card (one per small group) to wish the volunteer servers well and thank them for their service.

Attach one card to each bag of biscuits and deliver them fresh after school. Be sure to take a few pictures of the volunteers holding the bags to show the children the next day! This civic literacy project is an excellent way for students to develop their inner beauty in caring for others and live the mantra from the book: "Sometimes when you're surrounded by dirt, CJ, you're a better witness for what's beautiful" (unnumbered page).

Additional Activities

We can facilitate our students' process in taking action for social justice in many ways. Such activities provide real-world connections to the purpose of using literacy (written and visual) to effect change in a community and empower all citizens. Here are a few general activities that apply to a variety of issues found in modern picture books:

Poster Power

Students pair up to make posters about an issue to develop awareness among their school peers. For example, issues related to pollution and the urban environment could be addressed by having students create posters that encourage friends to recycle materials and throw trash in appropriate waste containers.

Take it a step further by having students collect recycled materials to bring to school for a special Earth Art Project Day: teachers would take time during the day to have their classes visit the art room or other multipurpose room to browse the found objects, bring them back to the classroom, and create unique works of art using the recycled materials. Encourage considerations of color, texture, and composition among students as they arrange their recycled objects.

Share the Warmth

After reading a picture book about homeless populations, such as *Way Home* (Hathorn, 1994) or *Fly Away Home* (Bunting, 1991), create an awareness among students for helping homeless people keep warm in winter months by having the students organize a hat/mitten/scarf collection campaign. Students research the needs of the area, create flyers, and set up collection stations around their school for a set period of time.

Discuss how to create flyers in terms of visual literacy: choose the colors intentionally to convey warmth and love: reds, oranges, bright yellows; use thick, stable lines (horizontal) to convey support and strength in unity; consider the overall composition of the text and illustrations on their flyers and/or posters, too.

Thinking of You

After reading a book such as *One Zillion Valentines* (Modell, 1987), in which two boys decide to make Valentine cards for all members of their community, teach the students to create Valentines (or "thinking of you" cards) to give to a local homeless shelter for distribution to its clients during meal time. This is another authentic reading/writing activity, because students are writing for a real audience: the recipients of the cards.

FINAL THOUGHTS

This chapter examined visual literacy through an exploration of Christian Robinson's illustrations for *Last Stop on Market Street* (de la Peña, 2015). This picture book serves as an example for teachers to build their knowledge of visual literacy and apply it to the use of other picture books in the classroom.

Matt de la Peña's book is an excellent example of one that is culturally specific, and it is important for teachers to build classroom libraries with such books so that all students will see themselves and others in their communities reflected in the literature they read for school.

Placing books in the library is only the beginning. Teachers should also "read" the illustrations in order to develop their own voices in leading their students to interpret and discuss the visual elements, as well as the emotional and sociocultural issues presented to the readers. Without teachers' instruction about how to interpret the visual elements and symbols, children will likely miss these key components in developing their visual literacy (Prior, Willson, & Martinez, 2012).

Beginning readers need to spend time reading quality literature that enables them to personally connect with the wider world while also guiding them in constructing knowledge and in taking action within their communities. Table 8.2 is a list of culturally responsive and specific picture books by award-winning authors and illustrators that serves as a resource for teachers to use in building their classroom libraries.

The list includes notations regarding key visual elements and/or social issues that dominate the illustrations of each book. This list is just a sampling of the plethora of award-winning, high-quality, culturally specific picture books available to readers. In addition, teachers should seek out additional books that will assist them in developing other authentic activities and classroom discussions that reflect each book's social issues.

Table 8.2.   Culturally Responsive Picture Books

Title, Author, and Illustrator	Social Issue/Topic	Main Visual Element
Ben's Trumpet, Rachel Isadora	Growing up in an urban environment in the mid-twentieth century	Line: especially diagonals used to convey anxiety, but also straight to convey quiet sense of security. Color: black-and-white illustrations reflect the art deco design of this book's era.
Tar Beach, Faith Ringgold	Urban family life; working-class issues	Color: bright cheerful colors to reflect hope and family joy despite facing financial difficulties. Symbolism: the quilt border of the author's original quilt art (which this story is based on) surrounds each page, reinforcing the security of family love.
Grandfather's Journey, Allen Say	Immigration from Japan to America across the	Color: soft pastels reflect faded, loving memories of

generations—defining a sense of home in both countries and connection to author's grandfather

the author's grandfather, while bright colors convey joyful moments in life, too.

Hot City, Barbara Joosse and Gregory Christie

Urban life: children visit their local library to escape the heat outside and discover adventure through literature

Shape: heads, bodies are all rounded, indicating natural beauty and warmth/love.
Symbolism: Heads are drawn much larger in proportion to bodies. Indicates wisdom, control, rule, intelligence, and "the seat of life-force and the soul and its power" (Cooper, 1978, p. 80). *Notice that Joe's shirt is yellow with a red book on it, while Mimi's shirt is blue with thin white stripes: primary colors = prime importance.

The Keeping Quilt, Patricia Polacco

Immigration from Russia; quilt symbolizes the love that connects several generations of the author's family and her Jewish heritage.

Color: Polacco uses color (especially red) to emphasize her great-gramma and the quilt made from relatives' clothing. The bright-red babushka became the quilt's border: red symbolizes many elements, including love, joy, passion, energy, health, and even the bridal torch or fire (see Cooper, 1978).

H.o.r.s.e.: A Game of Basketball and Imagination, Christopher Myers

Friendship: Two friends challenge each other to wildly imaginative basketball shots while playing HORSE on an outdoor urban court.

Color: both characters wear one of the primary colors, conveying their key roles in this story.
Line: exaggerated length of arms suggests their power and strength. The directionality of the arms guides the reader's eye to the important events, locations, and general progression of the story.

A Bike Like Sergio's, Maribeth Boelts and Noah Jones	Family life/difficult decisions: A boy sees money fall from a woman's purse and wants to use it to buy his own bike because his family cannot afford one.	Color: especially the blue-gray background in Ruben's room when he believes he lost the money and cannot buy the bike. This somber color continues with rain outside as he looks for the money and feels guilty about how he found it. The colors brighten when he returns the money to its owner.
Abuela, Arthur Dorros and Elisa Kleven	Familial love/urban life conveyed through the eyes of a Hispanic girl and her grandmother (*abuela*); includes text in Spanish	Color: bright, bold colors depict Rosalba and her *abuela*, while a combination of bright and pastel colors depicts the city. The double-spread illustrations of the colorful city provide the reader with a treasure trove of people and places to see. This mirrors the main characters' love of their city and their joy in visiting many places.
Yo! Yes? Richard Jackson and Chris Raschka	Friendship across cultures	Line: thick outlines of both characters; diagonals to convey excitement and strength in newfound friendship, especially when the lines of the characters' stances lean in toward each other as the story progresses.
The Other Side, Jacqueline Woodson and E. B. Lewis	Pre–civil rights era depiction of racial tensions when two young girls who live on opposite sides of a fence, one white, one black, gradually get to know each other.	Line: the fence is prominent in most illustrations, and it is made with strong, horizontal lines (with slight angle for perspective). Symbolism: the fence is positioned in the background on the first illustration and is gradually drawn closer to the foreground as the story progresses until, just when the two girls finally

introduce themselves, the fence dominates the front and center of the illustration. It gradually recedes into the background (becomes less important) until it becomes obscured by the addition of more friends who sit on the fence.

Smoky Night, Eve Bunting and David Diaz	Urban life/riots: a boy and his mom learn to value their neighbors' friendship as they endure the Los Angeles riot.	Texture: Diaz uses found-object collage on pages containing text to convey items looted in the riot, as well as tangible evidence of urban elements. The texture awakens within the reader a sense of presence and connection to the events of the riot. Color: Dark colors are used in paintings of people on facing pages. By the second half of the story, when the characters are safe in a shelter, the colors become bright and cheerful.
Apple Pie 4th of July, Janet Wong and Margaret Chodos-Irvine	Immigration: first-generation girl questions her parents' decision to keep their Chinese food store open on Independence Day.	Line: directionality of sidewalk leads reader's eye toward the parade. Symbolism: main character's stance and position block the story's progress during the first half of the book by facing to the left as if blocking the reader from turning the page. This matches her opposition to her parents' decision to make Chinese food to sell on Independence Day.
Something Beautiful, Sharon Dennis Wyeth and Chris Soentpiet	Urban life: a young girl searches for beauty in her neighborhood and finds it exists in many forms.	Color: dark colors convey the main character's somber outlook on the dirty landscape of her neighborhood. When she gets to school and learns

the word "beautiful," the colors become bright and cheerful.

Line: thick, sharp diagonals in first half of book convey anxiety and fear, especially the crosshatched chain-link fence that crisscrosses the main character's body when she runs past an alley.

Shape: circular shape of the jump rope and her friend's beaded necklaces convey infinite joy in the small beauties of her friends and family.

Hot Day on Abbott Avenue, Karen English and Javaka Steptoe	Urban life and friendship: two friends are angry with each other, but eventually make up during a hot summer day in the city.	Texture: cut paper and found-object collage create a three-dimensional effect, inviting the reader onto Abbott Avenue and into the events of the hot day. Color: Soft colors in earth tones, in both clothing and background, create a soothing sense despite the tension of two friends' argument. Shape: globular shape created by double-dutch jump-roping conveys continuity of friendship.
Thunder Boy, Jr., Sherman Alexie and Yuyi Morales	Familial love: a young boy is named after his father, but wants a name that gives him his own identity.	Texture: digital color created by the illustrator's use of rotted wood and clay creates a deeper dimension to the art, which reflects the deeper dimension of Thunder Boy, Jr., and his desire to be his own person. Color: bold primary colors throughout, with background colors that convey mood—especially when Thunder Boy, Jr., screams, "I hate my name!" Here the illustrator uses

bold blue, bright pink, and
deep red to convey anger.

CHILDREN'S BOOKS CITED

Alexie, S. (2016). *Thunder Boy, Jr.* New York: Little, Brown & Co.
Boelts, M. (2016). *A bike like Sergio's.* Somerville, MS: Candlewick Press.
Bunting, E. (1991). *Fly away home.* New York: Clarion.
———. (1994). *Smoky night.* San Diego, CA: Harcourt Brace & Co.
de la Peña, M. (2015). *Last stop on Market Street.* New York: G. P. Putnam and Sons.
Dorros, A. (1991). *Abuela.* New York: Dutton Children's Books.
English, K. (2004). *Hot day on Abbott Avenue.* New York: Clarion.
Hathorn, L. (1994). *Way home.* New York: Knopf Books for Young Readers.
Isadora, R. (1979). *Ben's trumpet.* New York: Greenwillow Books.
Joosse, B. (2004). *Hot city.* New York: Philomel.
Modell, F. (1987). *One zillion Valentines.* New York: Greenwillow Books.
Myers, C. (2012). *H.o.r.s.e.: A game of basketball and imagination.* New York: Egmont.
Polacco, P. (1988). *The keeping quilt.* New York: Aladdin Paperbacks.
Raschka, C. (1993). *Yo! Yes?* New York: Orchard Books.
Ringgold, F. (1990). *Tar beach.* New York: Crown Publishers.
Say, A. (1993). *Grandfather's journey.* New York: Houghton Mifflin.
Wong, J. (2002). *Apple pie 4th of July.* San Diego, CA: Harcourt.
Woodson, J. (2001). *The other side.* New York: G. P. Putnam's Sons.
Wyeth, S. D. (1998). *Something beautiful.* New York: Bantam Doubleday Dell.

REFERENCES

Cooney, B. (1988). Remarks made at a symposium, "Ways of saying, ways of knowing: Art for all ages." New England Reading Association Annual Conference, Portland, Maine.
Cooper, J. C. (1978). *An illustrated encyclopedia of traditional symbols.* London: Thames & Hudson, Ltd.
Epstein, S. (2014). *Teaching civic literacy projects: Student engagement with social problems grades 4–12.* New York: Teachers College Press.
Fleming, J., Catapano, S., Thompson, C. M., & Ruvalcaba Carillo, S. (2016). *More mirrors in the classroom: Using urban children's literature to increase literacy.* Lanham, MD: Rowman & Littlefield.
Gay, G. (2010). *Culturally responsive teaching: Theory, research, and practice* (2nd ed.). New York: Teachers College Press.
Hassett, D., & Curwood, J. S. (2009). Theories and practices of multimodal education: The instructional dynamics of picture books and primary classrooms. *The Reading Teacher, 63(4),* 270–82.
Hollie, S. (2011). *Culturally and linguistically responsive teaching and learning: Classroom practices for student success.* Huntington Beach, CA: Shell Education.
Kiefer, B. (1995). *The potential of picture books: From visual literacy to aesthetic understanding.* New York: Merrill.
Nodelman, P. (1996). *The pleasures of children's literature* (2nd ed.). New York: Longman.
Perkins, M. (2009). Straight talk on race: Challenging stereotypes in kids' books. *School Library Journal, 55(4),* 28–32.
Prior, L. A., Willson, A., & Martinez, M. (2012). Picture this: Visual literacy as a pathway to character understanding. *The Reading Teacher, 66(3),* p. 195–206.
Rosenblatt, L. (1994). The transactional theory of reading and writing. In R. Ruddell, M. Rapp Ruddell, & H. Singer (Eds.), *Theoretical models and processes of reading* (4th ed.) (pp. 1057–92). Newark, DE: International Reading Association.

————. (1995). *Literature as exploration* (5th ed.). New York: Modern Language Association.
Schwarcz, J., & Schwarcz, C. (1991). *The picture book comes of age: Looking at childhood through the art of illustration.* Chicago: American Library Association.
Yenawine, P. (1997). Thoughts on visual literacy. In J. Flood, S. B. Heath, and D. Lapp (Eds.), *Handbook of research on teaching literacy through the communicative and visual arts: A project of the International Reading Association* (pp. 845–46). New York: Routledge.

Index

About the Editors

Barbara Purdum-Cassidy is a clinical assistant professor in the Department of Curriculum and Instruction at Baylor University. She currently teaches elementary language arts methods courses to preservice teachers and graduate students in the Department of Curriculum and Instruction. Cassidy has almost three decades of combined experiences at the elementary, middle, undergraduate, and graduate teaching levels. She is coeditor of *Culturally Affirming Literacy Practices for Elementary Students* (2016). She has also published several research articles that examine best practices for teaching urban students. Some of these works include *Beyond Basic Instruction: Effective Civic Literacy Instruction in Urban School Settings* (2016); *An Analysis of the Ways in Which Preservice Teachers Integrate Children's Literature in Mathematics* (2015); *and What Are They Asking? An Analysis of the Questions Planned by Prospective Teachers When Integrating Literature in Mathematics* (2015). She is currently conducting a multiyear study examining the effects of inquiry-based instruction on urban students' reading and writing achievement. Her current research interests include creating urban literacy initiatives to advance student academic outcomes, inquiry-based instruction, and preservice teachers' beliefs and efficacy for teaching writing and inquiry.

Lakia M. Scott is an assistant professor of urban education and literacy at Baylor University. She currently teaches diversity education and literacy methods courses to preservice teachers and graduate students in the Department of Curriculum and Instruction. Scott has over a decade of combined experiences at the elementary, secondary, undergraduate, and graduate teaching levels. She is the coeditor of *Culturally Affirming Literacy Practices for Elementary Students* (2016). She has also published several research articles that align with best practices for teaching African American and Hispanic/ Latino(a) students. Some of these works include *Linguistic Hegemony Today: Recommendations for Eliminating Language Discrimination* (2017), *English as a Gatekeeper: A Conversation of Linguistic Capital and American schools* (2014), and *Micro-aggressions and African American and Hispanic Students in Urban Schools: A Call for Culturally Affirming Education* (2013). She is currently conducting research on national reading and language intervention programs, specifically the Children's Defense Fund (CDF) Freedom Schools Program, which is a literacy program geared toward social action and advocacy issues that directly affect youth while also curbing summer learning loss. She is the inaugural executive director of the CDF Freedom Schools at Baylor University program. Under her research framework of increasing educational access and opportunities for minoritized youth, she primarily examines urban literacy initiatives that advance student academic outcomes, multicultural awareness and perspectives in teacher education programs, and Historically Black Colleges and Universities as a gateway for first-generation student success.

About the Contributors

Lauren Bagwell received her BS in secondary education and an MA in curriculum and instruction from Baylor University. As a spoken word poet, Bagwell is passionate about the role poetry can play as a pedagogical tool in the social studies classroom. As an educator, Bagwell aims to create a democratic classroom that empowers students to share their stories and take action to not only learn about history, but to also make history.

Brooke Blevins is an associate professor of social studies education and associate chair of the Department of Curriculum and Instruction at Baylor University. Dr. Blevins teaches both undergraduate and graduate courses in secondary education, social studies education, and multicultural education. Her research focuses on social studies education as a means to prepare active and engaged citizens. She is also interested in how to educate and empower young people to become active civic participants through participation in action civics and digital technologies. Dr. Blevins also serves as the codirector for the iEngage Summer Civics Institute.

Mona M. Choucair is a senior lecturer at Baylor University. She teaches American Literature survey courses as well as an advanced grammar course in the English department and young adult literature and secondary English methods courses in the School of Education. She is an active member of the Council for College Teachers of English and the South Central Modern Language Association, and continues her annual role as an invited grader and question leader for the College Board, specifically in the Advanced Placement English language exams. Dr. Choucair is currently working on a book project that outlines the role of young adult literature in the traditional English curriculum used in secondary schools.

Meredith Dana earned her BS in education from Baylor University in 2016. She participated in the Undergraduate Research and Scholarly Achievement program under Dr. Lakia M. Scott and was accepted to present her research at national conferences as an undergraduate student. During her time as an undergraduate, she excelled in her student leadership positions, and discovered her calling to the field of student affairs. She is currently working toward her master's degree in educational administration with a concentration in student affairs administration and higher education at Texas A&M University. She works as a graduate assistant for a scholarship program serving first-generation college students, and hopes to continue working in college student access programs upon her graduation in May 2018.

Evan Ditmore holds a BA in English and MAEd in secondary education from Wayland Baptist University, in addition to a supplementary school principal certification. He has taught language arts to diverse students in Texas and New Mexico public schools. His experience with vulnerable adolescent populations at North Texas State Hospital ignited his interest in developing literacy strategies to confront the challenges facing nontraditional public school students who struggle with the fundamentals of reading.

Jacqueline Easley is the dean of the Division of Professional Studies at Carthage College in Kenosha, Wisconsin, where she also serves as an associate professor in the Department of Education. At Carthage, she teaches courses in the methods of teaching reading and language arts in both elementary and secondary classrooms, as well as courses in children's literature, and creative arts instruction. Dr. Easley is a former elementary teacher and assistant children's librarian. Her research interests include integrating children's literature across the curriculum, visual literacy, and culturally responsive literacy instruction.

Nancy P. Gallavan is a professor of teacher education at the University of Central Arkansas. She specializes in classroom assessments, cultural competence, and social studies education. With 160+ publications including *Developing Performance-based Assessments*, *Navigating Cultural Competence*, *Secrets to Success in Social Studies Classrooms*, *Secrets to Success in Elementary School Classrooms*, and *Annual Editions: Multicultural Education*, Nancy is active in the American Educational Research Association, National Association for Multicultural Education, National Council for the Social Studies, Association of Teacher Educators, and Southeastern Regional Association of Teacher Educators, serving as ATE president in 2013–2014 and coeditor of the *ATE Yearbook* (2012–2018). Nancy is an ATE Distinguished Member and a KDP Eleanor Roosevelt Legacy Chapter Member.

Amanda Gardner earned her BA and MA in English and her single subject clear credential in English from California State University, Sacramento (CSUS). She spent nineteen years teaching high school English in various socioeconomic public school settings, and has worked as adjunct English faculty at University of Nevada, Las Vegas. Her current areas of focus are media literacy and the current endangered state of public education.

Karon LeCompte is an associate professor of curriculum and instruction with an emphasis in social studies education at Baylor University in Waco, Texas. She teaches classes in elementary social studies methods. Dr. Le-Compte's research interests include civics education, multicultural education, and teacher preparation. She works with teachers on civics education and law-related education.

Gloria Loring has been a classroom teacher for eight years in the Pulaski County Special School District (PCSSD). Honorably discharged after twenty years with the U.S. Army National Guard, she was selected to participate in the 2012–2013 Arkansas Leadership Academy Teacher Institute. Serving as site coordinator for the 21st Century After School Program, Gloria implemented the grant. She participated in the 2012 University of Central Arkansas National Council for Accreditation of Teacher Education (NCATE) review, and received the 2012 Southeastern Regional Association of Teacher Educators (SRATE) Post Bachelorette Award.

Margaret Thomson is a senior lecturer in the Department of Curriculum and Instruction at Baylor University. She teaches undergraduate elementary and literacy methods courses. Her current scholarship focuses on literacy development, research-based literacy instruction, and Montessori education.

Randy Wood is a professor of curriculum and instruction at Baylor University. He has written several books and numerous articles in professional journals. He has also directed the Center for Christian Education, and was named Educator of the Year by the Accreditation Commission of the Texas Association of Baptist Schools. Dr. Wood is the founder of the LEAF (Learning English Among Friends) adult literacy program.